Beggars'
Banquets

Beggars'
Banquets

Marlena Spieler

PIATKUS

First published in 1999 by
Judy Piatkus (Publishers) Ltd
5 Windmill Street, London W1P 1HF

The moral right of the author has been asserted

A catalogue record for this book is available from the British Library

ISBN 0–7499–1851–9

Designed by Paul Saunders
Photographs by Ian O'Leary
Home Economy by Virginia Alcock
Styling by Marian Price

Data capture & manipulation by Wyvern 21, Bristol
Printed and bound in Great Britain by
The Bath Press, Bath, Somerset

Contents

Preface

Hospitality – both giving and receiving – is one of life's greatest pleasures. Time spent with friends and acquaintances, sharing thoughtfully prepared food and delicious conversation, cocooned in the warmth of hospitality, is utterly reviving. Lingering at the table, filled with good food and drink, our spirits lifted by conversation and companionship, we are nourished in more ways than just by vitamins and minerals. Such an occasion imparts a sense of well-being, of belonging, indeed of civilization itself. After all, all animals eat; how many give dinner parties?

However, entertaining is hard work – all that shopping and chopping – and although the rewards for your efforts are great, what about the expense? It's a dilemma: I love to entertain lavishly; I want all who sit at my table to enjoy the freshest, tastiest, most interesting foods I can offer, but I also need to pay the mortgage and the bills and go on holiday. And my cat needs to eat, too.

I have therefore devised a system that allows me to have it all. Of course, having an accountant for a husband is a great help when it comes to creative shopping and budgeting. In fact, we have turned it into a game and a strategy: hunt for bargains, buy in season, search out discounts, and, occasionally, forage for free. I think it brings out our basic hunting instincts – few shopping expeditions are as exciting as hunting out and bagging that bargain. My daughter, too, has her own strategy: a busy medical student with a vegetarian boyfriend, she and her partner are often looking for dishes to make, parties to give and foods to prepare that are vegetarian and cheap enough to afford on a grant.

Our friends throughout Europe have lots of tips on how to save money at the table. Many of these are for excellent eating and only incidentally are thrifty too: foraging for wild asparagus and herbs; eating lots of beans and pulses; baking their own bread or making their own pasta. Thrift and frugality can be tasty and healthy, too. Of course, what is cheapest in one place can be a costly delicacy in another. Basil costs little in Italy, California or Provence, which means you can add lashings of homemade pesto to almost anything, but in London you count basil leaf by costly leaf. Asparagus and artichokes are expensive in Britain, cheaper and cheaper as one works their way south across Europe. In France, good bread is cheap; in Britain hard to find and dear. But then, I've bought Stilton, bangers, crumpets and marmalade in California – and you wouldn't believe what I paid for them!

This book is all about our little game, and the tips I've gathered along the way, but there are three very important things to remember. First, cutting corners on cost never *ever* means cutting corners on quality. In fact, many money-saving tips are also tips for excellent cooking and eating. Second, you do not need to be on a tight budget to entertain with frugality in mind. Keep track of your savings and donate it to your favourite charity – it'll give you an even warmer glow knowing that you and your guests are not the only ones benefiting from the evening. Finally, this collection of recipes, while designed to show you how to entertain as inexpensively as possible, is not austere. It is food for any time, not just when your purse strings need a bit of tightening.

If you have eaten at my table, I hope you will have felt cared for and deliciously fed. Don't tell anyone, but the chances are that it was very likely budget entertaining.

Acknowledgements

To: Leah, almost a doctor, always my little girl; Alan, my bargain hunting husband ('discount' is his favourite word).

To: Heather Rocklin and Rachel Winning, cheerful and enthusiastic editors; Borra Garson, agent and e-mailer par excellence; Helen Southall, attentive copy-editor.

To: Jon Harford; Gretchen of Paris and her poodle; Sue Kreitzman; Paula Levine ('cousin' and barter-mate); Fred and Mary Barclay; Alexa Stace; 'Kash' Taj; 'sweet' Lynne Meikle of Tate & Lyle (for showering me with sugar!); Philippa Davenport; Kathleen Griffen; Sri and Roger Owen (to sit at their table is a joy).

To: Amanda Hamilton and Tim Hemmeter; Rabbi Jason Gaber; Sandy Waks; Kamala Friedman; Jerome Freeman and Sheila Hannon; Dr Esther Novak and the Rev John Chendo; Nigel Patrick; Graham Ketteringham; Susie Morgenstern; Paul Richardson; Gianni and Pamela Parmigiani for all things Italian.

To: Pat and Sandra at Samson Travel; Crispin Burridge of Marks & Spencer; Asda, Somerfield, Tesco, Sainsbury's, Kwiksave and Budgens for a sampling of low-cost wines; Kikkoman for very fine soy sauce; Torz and Macatonia for the best coffee on this whole little island; Ben and Jerry's and Hill Station for sending us tubs of the best ice cream on this planet; Fortnum and Mason's; Judi Scott-Nunn and Claire Sawford; Claire Weight of Tony Mace Marketing; Bennett Opie Speciality Foods Ltd; Gareth Shannon at The Society of Authors; Paulo Ardisson (of John Burgess Imports) for enough beautiful capers to last a lifetime.

To: M. A. Mariner, Michael Bauer, Fran Irwin and my colleagues at the *San Francisco Chronicle*; all of the publications, television and radio programmes I have appeared in throughout the writing of this book.

To: parents Caroline and Izzy Smith; Aunt Estelle and Uncle Sy Opper; little cousins Melissa, Steven, Allison, Lexie and Jordan; Matthew, who really is our cousin, and his friend Brett Olenick, who just seems like he is; especially my grandmother Sophia Dubowsky who is legendary for 'Bachi's kitchen'.

To: my kitchen pals: Freud, pussy-cat extraordinaire, and Basil, the bunny.

Introduction

THE STRATEGY

Many food writers have addressed the subject of cooking on a budget – Mrs Beeton, for example (*Beeton's Penny Cookery Book*), and in 1942 M.F.K. Fisher wrote *How to Cook a Wolf* (that proverbial 'wolf at the door') as a guide to the economies necessitated by the rationing of the Second World War.

Everyone has their own tricks, but to cook abundant, interesting and very appealing food for guests, deliciously and healthfully too – that is the trick of Houdini.

Yet, as it was with Houdini, the difficulty is all illusion; although they might sound obvious, these little tricks work. Some are explained in this introductory chapter; others are scattered throughout the rest of the book.

Follow the Seasons

The most important way to cook well and spend little is to follow the seasons. In August, sweet red peppers, aubergines and courgettes will be cheaper than cabbage, potatoes and root vegetables, which are all traditionally thought of as 'cheap'. In spring, a nice bunch of fat asparagus just might be affordable enough to buy lavish amounts; in winter it will not. Don't underestimate this particular strategy: what is a hugely expensive dish to prepare out of season can cost almost nothing when the vegetables are at their peak.

Flexibility is your best friend. So, too, is knowing how to cook. A combination of the two will enable you to buy what is cheapest, make substitutions for ingredients that are unexpectedly pricey when you get to the market, and delight all who dine at your table.

Save Money on What Won't Show and Spend it on What Will

Never skimp on amounts of certain things when entertaining; it is the sense of being lavished with abundance that makes a guest feel special. As a guest, there is nothing better than to see a generously set table, and to know that it is all in your honour. (As a host, it's equally gratifying to know that you haven't made yourself bankrupt.)

One or two carefully chosen extravagances give a delightful sense of the special. Use small amounts – say, a few prawns scattered about, a drizzling of truffle oil, one slice of prosciutto chopped finely and used to garnish a plate of pasta – but use them where they are most visible. Serving a budget-minded dinner party means accomplishing a balance between saving money on what won't show and spending it on what will.

Barter

When your local supermarket has a discount on sausages, cream or cabbages, for example, buy more than you need and offer some to a friend or neighbour who might have a herb garden you can pick from, bake more bread than *they* need, or pick up bargains for you when they come across them.

Make the Most of Supermarket Offers

Supermarkets tend frequently to have offers on all sorts of things, including vegetables, dairy products, meat, poultry and fish. *Ask* for a discount when the sell-by date is approaching, or the aubergines look a bit the worse for wear.

Become familiar with the flavours of the various cheeses, yogurts, fromage frais, etc., so that you can use whichever one is priced best when you need it. Only buy the freshest of fish, but discounted meat and poultry are one of my entertaining mainstays – pop them into the freezer and take them out when you feel a party coming on. Having a stockpile of meats and poultry means a varied and interesting menu that scarcely hurts the wallet.

Concentrate on Flavour

To turn simple dishes into spectacular ones, you will need to splash out on a few items that are wonderful rather than cheap.

Olive oil
You should always have a good extra virgin olive oil on your shelf; it will turn even the simplest of vegetables into a Mediterranean feast.

Ethnic flavours

Soy, sesame oil, lemon grass, hot pepper seasonings, pesto, etc., all excite the palate and transform humble foods. They can be expensive, so assemble them one or two at a time as you do your usual shopping.

Fresh herbs

Fresh herbs add great aroma and fragrance; eating a meal flavoured with lots of fresh herbs is almost like walking through a scented garden. Unfortunately, many, such as basil, chervil and tarragon, are pricey when sold, as they often are, in little packets. Look for packets that are reduced in price because they are approaching their sell-by date. They'll be fine if used that night or the next.

Try growing your own herbs on a windowsill or tiny plot outside your door. It not only gives you a good supply of herbs, but makes a relaxing, rewarding hobby.

Alternatively, go ethnic, and purchase thyme in bunches from a Caribbean shop; coriander and flat-leaf parsley from an Indian shop; mature rocket, dill and mint from a Cypriot grocery, if you are lucky enough to have such shops in your area.

Don't Neglect the Simple Things

Bread

Good bread is indispensable to a good meal, but sometimes finding it can be daunting. Some supermarkets sell excellent French bread; buy it when it is on offer and keep it in your freezer. It will bake in the oven into almost bakery-fresh bread (give it a little spray with water before you bake it if it seems dry). Pitta, naan, flour tortillas and other ethnic breads also freeze extremely well.

Stale bread can be a treasure for your entertaining kitchen, too. Slice it into crostini or croûtes, layer it into bread puddings, or whirl it in your blender or food processor into breadcrumbs; and if you've no machinery for the task, grate the stale bread on a hand grater, *et voilà* – lovely light breadcrumbs.

Grains and legumes

Interesting and inexpensive, grains and legumes are chic, too! A big pot of simmering wheat grains or barley makes a rustic Tuscan soup, or, when cold, can become a surprisingly refreshing salad. Beans and lentils of every variety are marvellous paired with grains or meats.

Fruit

Dessert can be a problem as so many really delicious desserts cost a fortune to create. Good quality chocolate, cream, nuts and other ingredients can eat into your budget. Fruit in season is your best bet, and will be at its most delicious and cheapest when very ripe. This slightly over-the-hill fruit can be marvellous mashed into mousse, roasted and caramelized into a compote, frozen into a sorbet or baked into a tart.

Check out Street Markets

Haunt the street markets late in the day when prices are being reduced and you can buy all sorts of fruits and vegetables that you otherwise wouldn't want to pay for. If you are feeling particularly brave, shop the markets for discards as they are closing. This is hair-raising and unpredictable, and, while not for everyone, is deliciously cheap and thrilling.

Keep an Eye on Your Resources

Only you know how much you can spend on your gathering. I have not given specific costs per recipe or per person in this book, as the cost of the same dish will vary considerably depending on where you purchase the ingredients and what time of year it is. You'll need to choose with an eye towards your own resources.

This book is not about cheap foods *per se*, but about getting the most for your money, and entertaining deliciously and lavishly for the smallest amount. If you feel that entertaining is too expensive to consider, remember that having guests over for a meal costs far less than going to a restaurant. Moreover, the rewards of hospitality come not only from the pleasant afterglow of welcoming others into your home and everyone having a wonderful time, but there is an added bonus: your friends will invite you to *their* house next time.

One warning: there is entertaining on a budget and then there is the point at which it is best to forget it. If you can't afford a few simpler foods and the relaxation to serve it with, wait until you are better able to do it. Entertaining should bring you pleasure, not be an ordeal.

THE STORECUPBOARD

What you keep in your storecupboard reflects and creates the style of the food you serve. A well-stocked storecupboard makes it possible for you to prepare exciting, imaginative dishes effortlessly.

Oils and Fats

Most supermarkets carry a wide range of excellent quality olive oils. Be sure to choose extra virgin, from a shop that does not store it on the top shelf where the sunlight reaches it and dissipates its delicious flavour and goodness. Plain olive oil (pure olive oil) is okay for frying, but avoid any of the highly hyped blends of vegetable and pure olive oil – they have none of the goodness or flavour of extra virgin olive oil.

Butter is an excellent ingredient, but since we spread too much on our bread if it is available, I now buy it only for entertaining – this saves both on pennies and on unwanted fats in our diet. I have little use for margarine, so I recommend avoiding it.

Dry Goods

Flours (plain and self-raising, white and brown), cornflour, sugars (including coarse brown cubes), good tea and the best coffee you can find will make entertaining a delight. Stale bread is one of the most useful things to have in the frugal kitchen: grate it into crumbs; slice and toast it for croûtons; cut it thinly and fry it for crostini, etc.

Salt and Pepper

It is amazing how much difference good quality salt and pepper can make to the flavour of a dish. Black, white, green, pink and Szechuan peppercorns add a distinctively different peppery flavour and smell; vary your pepper to match your meal.

Sea salt, especially coarse grains or flakes, is my salt of choice. It gives the mineral scent of the sea and seems to enhance food rather than just make it salty.

Condiments and Other Flavourings

Mustards are one of the things I collect when I travel, especially in France. I also always have tahini, vinegars (especially balsamic and various wine vinegars), capers, olives, sesame oil and soy sauce, good quality mayonnaise, hoisin sauce, tandoori/curry paste, hot chilli oil and rice vinegar.

Stocks are good to keep to hand. Hot sauces of the Mexican variety are delicious, and Tabasco adds pure, sour heat, a few drops enhancing almost any dish. Chipotle chillies, with their smoky flavour and scent, are always on my shelf. Dried, they keep forever and make a good spicy barbecue sauce. Chutney and Indian pickles are also great storecupboard items. And, I confess, I do keep a bottle of ketchup to hand. It is good in Chinese and Malaysian or Thai dishes, as well as in barbecue sauce, and it does occasionally stray on to my plate of scrambled eggs or chips!

Herbs and Spices

With the delicious exception of some of the stronger flavoured herbs (bay leaves, sage, oregano, thyme and, to a lesser extent, dill and mint) and various mixtures (such as herbes de Provence), dried herbs are not so fragrant and flavourful as the sweet-smelling, strong-tasting fresh ones. Buy them still growing in little pots, if you can, and keep a garden on your windowsill. If, like me, you do not possess green fingers, make friends with neighbours who do.

Spices are the seeds of flavouring plants, while herbs are the leafy green tops. Unlike herbs and their enhancing freshness, spices are at their best dried. They last longest and keep their aroma and flavour most intact when purchased whole and ground as needed. Spices should be bought in smallish amounts that will be used within six months or so.

Paprika, cumin (both ground and seeds), cardamom, coriander (both ground and seeds), cayenne pepper, dried red chilli flakes, ground turmeric, ground ginger, allspice, whole nutmeg, cloves, cinnamon (both sticks and ground), mild red chilli powder, fennel seeds, curry/garam masala and five-spice powder are all spices that will flavour your foods over and over again. Although it might not seem like a budget ingredient, saffron is lovely to keep to hand, while sesame, caraway and poppy seeds are marvellous for coating bread dough for a crusty, seedy loaf.

Dried Fruits and Nuts

I always keep a supply of the following: raisins, sultanas, prunes, apricots, walnuts (either halves, whole or pieces), peanuts, cashews, pistachio nuts, hazelnuts, almonds, desiccated coconut and creamed coconut chunks.

Canned and Bottled Foods

I would never be without: tomatoes (whole and chopped) and/or passata; various beans (black, soya, pinto, red kidney, white cannellini, chickpeas); tuna/salmon, sardines, anchovies; sweetcorn; preserves such as strawberry jam, apricot jam, honey, marmalade, maple syrup, peanut butter; good quality alcoholic drinks, such as *vin ordinaire* (white, rosé and red), dry sherry for soups and stir-fries, brandy, port, rum, beer; juices such as orange, cranberry and tomato.

Pasta and Grains

These are among the most useful storecupboard items, and should include a selection of dried pasta shapes: long strands, short, squat, chunky pastas, flat noodles, hollow tubular pastas, tiny pastina and orzo. A selection of different types of rice, including white and brown, with jasmine, basmati (for Asian dishes) and arborio (for risotto) are also essential. Couscous and polenta add diversity to the menu, and whole wheat grains, bulgar wheat and barley are always welcome and cost little.

Frozen Foods

Spinach, sweetcorn, broad beans, peas, puff and filo pastry, flour and corn tortillas, pesto (better than in a jar), homemade stock (or bones to make stock with) are always in my freezer, as are bread, wonton wrappers, fresh pasta, sausages, meat and whatever else has been sold at a discount and will freeze well.

SHOPPING AND EATING WITH THE SEASONS

A salad of ripe tomatoes, glistening with freshness and sweet juices, will be a near-impossibility in the winter; if you buy a nice big bag and ripen them on your windowsill, they will cost you dearly, half will rot and the rest will disappoint. Peppers, aubergines, courgettes, strawberries, etc., are available all year round, but buy them in the winter and they will take up an indecent chunk of your food budget. This is to be expected.

Less expected is the fact that some of the humbler vegetables, traditionally thought of as cheap, can also be quite expensive out of season. This includes potatoes, cabbage, beetroot and leeks. At these times, it's cheaper to go for the Mediterranean vegetables, though it does depend where on the calendar you find yourself. Thankfully, carrots and onions seem to be reasonably priced all the time but, unhappily, other vegetables seem always to be expensive. The best way of shopping is according to the season, and cost is usually a good guide; whatever is in season will be the cheapest and, most likely, the tastiest.

Spring

The vegetables of spring are often delicate, and always eagerly awaited after a long and cold winter of roots and other hearty produce.

Asparagus and strawberries are my finest reassurance that the world is really renewing itself and that warmer weather is on its way. Young greens, such as tender salad mixtures, watercress and rocket, and herbs such as tarragon, chervil, chives, parsley and mint, are all suddenly there: on the supermarket shelves, at the greengrocer's, in the garden!

In some areas of the world, you'll find spring garlic, the young shoots of garlic eaten as spring onions. To grow your own, simply plant whole cloves of garlic in a little pot with the pointed end turned up, just covered with soil. Leave on a windowsill in the direct sun and wait for it to sprout. Use the sprouts like spring onion tops or chives.

New potatoes, broccoli and young beetroot are in abundance in the spring, along with leeks and avocados. Apples, pears and the last of the citrus fruits are still to be found, as is pineapple. Rhubarb might show up, too, if you are lucky, as will fresh broad beans and tiny peas.

Summer

From June until the end of September, fruits and vegetables are at their cheapest, lushest and most delicious. Now is the time for the ripest toma-

Opposite: Roasted Summer Vegetables and Pesto 'Pizza' (page 34)
Opposite page 9: Goats' Cheese Crostini with Beetroot 'Caviar' (page 38)

toes of the year, and for sweet fragrant basil to make your own pesto or to toss into salads and soups.

Courgettes, aubergines, thin green beans and fat runner beans, corn on the cob and globe artichokes are all abundant for barbecuing or roasting, steaming, tossing with pasta or baking into gratins; cucumbers, tomatoes, celery, radishes and peppers are all juicy and refreshing for summer salads. Gratins of aubergine and/or courgettes are delicious at this time; baked with sunny tomatoes that can be eaten at room temperature instead of hot, or packed up for an impromptu picnic.

Cherries, berries, nectarines and peaches, melons, plums and currants of all colours – red, white and black – fill the summer supermarket shelves. Mangoes are imported from India and Pakistan; try the honey mango – though not cheap it is exquisite, and a small amount will go further towards thrilling your guests than all of the ingredients that go into a rich dessert.

As the summer winds down to its sultry ending, a wide variety of sweet-fleshed melons come on to the market, and they are often very reasonably priced when they are truly ripe. If they are flavourful but mushy, purée them and freeze them into a fragrant sorbet; if they are firm, serve them with a drizzle of port or armagnac, or splurge and accompany them with a plate of prosciutto.

Autumn

Summer's lushness disappears as the leaves turn golden and russet, but much of the fresh summer produce is still in abundance. Aubergines and peppers are in the last throes of their peak season now, as are tomatoes. The first hearty orange-fleshed squashes and pumpkins of the winter are coming on to the market or ripening in your garden. Courgettes are numerous and cheap, and marrow is coming into its own. An underrated vegetable, marrow can taste just like courgette and a single one of these monster vegetables can last and last and last.

Slightly bitter greens, such as frisée, radicchio and chicory, are readily available now, and are perfect for the heartier salads that the cooler season dictates.

Exotic and wild mushrooms, such as ceps, morels, 'trompettes de la mort' and chanterelles, are pricey unless you are a hunter or they are on offer at the supermarket, but plain, black, flat specimens and common cultivated mushrooms are all reasonable now. Swedes, carrots and parsnips tend to be endearingly cheap at this time, too, and summery lettuces and herbs are still on every shelf.

Pomegranates, persimmons (both the traditional squishy kind and the firm 'sharon fruit' or 'fuyu' type), sweet figs, and the last of the black-berries ... then there are pears and apples, the two most glorious fruits of autumn and winter. Try to explore and sample the wide variety of traditional English apples – winey, sweet, juicy or crisp. Few fruits are more satisfying or a bigger bargain come the onset of autumn and winter.

Winter

'Comforting' is the word for winter food, and what is more comforting than those root vegetables, rich and hearty, and full of fibre and satis-faction? Potatoes, turnips and swedes, Jerusalem artichokes, carrots and parsnips are all abundant. I also adore celeriac, a knobbly vegetable also known as root celery or celery root.

All members of the cabbage family are cheap and healthful, and under-rated in the deliciousness department. Green, curly-leafed, red, white or black, pointed or sprouting, cabbage is great for soups and stir-fries, to stuff, shred raw for salads or to toss into curries or stews. Chinese cab-bage, also known as Nappa cabbage or Chinese leaves, gives a Chinese flavour to stir-fries with small amounts of meat and/or tofu, and is lovely simmered in stock for a simple and very authentic soup. Broccoli, cauli-flower, kale and Brussels sprouts are all members of the cabbage family, too, and they are indeed fresh, abundant, delicious and cheap at this time of year. Chestnuts are available, and are delicious roasted over an open fire, or shelled and added to stuffings or soups.

Pears and apples are in abundance, as are imports such as pineapples, cranberries and lychees. Nuts in their shells and citrus fruits are all tra-ditionally imported fresh for the winter holiday season, and they make wonderful foods for our winter tables.

CREATING THE MENU

Plan your menu around your guests' tastes and delights as well as the market seasons, keeping in mind any allergies or pet hates. If your guests like basic food, keep the menu somewhat undaunting; if they like exotic flavours, serve them the special delicacies that you want to share with kindred spirits. Remember, though, that even those who might claim to favour simple foods often find it stimulating to have their tastes and senses stretched.

The first course sets the scene. Just *having* a first course emphasizes that this is a party. Everyone's tastebuds will be at their keenest at the beginning of the meal, so make a big impression and let the first course be thrilling. Raw vegetable salads, a tableful of tapas or meze, a bowl of soup perfumed with a few drops of truffle oil (yes, this is economical luxury, it really is) – all stimulate and encourage socialization and conviviality. A bowl of soup or pasta, Italian style, is not only delicious, but it reminds us of time spent in that amazing country, the charm of the language, lifestyle and food. Ditto a warm salad: very French, it stretches exotic or luxury ingredients (duck, for example) with a handful of greens.

Theming a menu can be fun. In the past, a heatwave has inspired me to have a 'surfin' safari' picnic in my rooftop garden, *Cinco de Mayo* (a Mexican holiday) usually moves me to hold a fiesta of Mexican cooking and eating, and any trip to the Mediterranean inspires my dinner parties for weeks (no, make that months) to follow.

Heavy desserts, no matter how sweet your tooth is, are not a treat when eaten on an overfull stomach, so if you're planning a hearty or very rich dessert, cut back on the rest of the meal. Many people feel 'unfinished' without a sweet ending: sometimes the simplicity of a plate of ripe pears and another of plain dark chocolate squares makes a satisfying dessert that doesn't overburden either the body or the pocket.

What to Drink?

Wine, beer, fruit juices and bottled waters can all eat into the entertaining budget, but you cannot have a dinner party, brunch, or any entertaining event, without them. Most people bring a bottle of wine or other tipple, but you need to have a few bottles of back-up drink just in case. Many supermarket chains offer good quality, very reasonably priced wines, with blurbs fixed on the shelf describing each wine's properties to help you choose.

I've included recipes for a couple of cocktails and a couple of fruit smoothies, which I hope you will enjoy.

A note about the recipes
Unless otherwise stated, the recipes in the following chapters serve six people, a number that seems perfect for entertaining.

Nibbles, Dips and Drinks

1

Nibbles, Dips and Drinks

...bright flavours and colours, fun to nibble on with drinks and intriguing enough to set the mood...

Nibbles, Dips and Drinks

PARTY food should be full of bright flavours and colours, fun to nibble on with drinks, and intriguing enough to set the mood for the rest of the evening. Food that is exciting and lively encourages good conversation, relaxed guests and a good party.

You may be having an all-cocktail and nibbles party and want an abundant supply of zesty foods to dip into throughout the evening, or you might be serving a proper meal afterwards and want to offer just enough to pique your guests' appetites for the even more intriguing delights that await at the table.

Crisp crackery things, bowls of homemade toasted seeds, popcorn or nuts and olives are all good for munching while sipping glasses of wine. Raw vegetables and dips are great party fare as the vegetables are fresh and light, the dips a bit indulgent and guests can help themselves as they wish.

Tostadas, pizzettas, or Anti-vampire Garlic–Pesto Bread are delicious, as are bite-sized pieces of anything small and savoury such as meze dishes and tapas.

If you're not convinced that homemade nibbles are worth the effort, keep in mind that they are more reasonably priced than snacks sold in shops, which are usually deep-fried things that dull the palate and, I am convinced, dull the party, too.

Popcorn

You can buy popcorn already popped: in the cinema it smells irresistible but costs too much; in chic little packages from speciality food shops it costs even more. Or you can pop it at home – a bag of the hard kernels costs little and pops up to mountains of snowy, crunchy satisfaction.

◆ Put a tiny amount of vegetable oil in a deep, heavy saucepan that has a tight-fitting lid. You only need just enough to cover the bottom of the pan with a little bit of a slick, say about 1mm/¹⁄₁₆in.

◆ Pour in enough popcorn kernels to form a single layer in the bottom of the pan. Cover and place over a medium-high heat. Shake the pan every so often when you hear the kernels beginning to pop, without removing the lid (or popcorn will shoot all over the place, and not only will this stop the popping process, but it is dangerous besides – a popping kernel could hit you in the eye!).

◆ The popcorn will be ready when the popping sounds stop. Remove it from the heat and let it sit for a moment with the lid on so that no errant popping corn flies about the kitchen, then remove the lid and pour the popcorn into a big bowl.

◆ Any kernels left unpopped are called 'old maids'. Discard them – they can break your teeth. Sometimes popcorn burns slightly; to prevent this, keep it moving by shaking the pan frequently, and keep the heat just hot enough to pop the corn without burning it.

◆ Popcorn is traditionally drizzled with a bit of melted butter and sprinkled with salt; some add sugar but I think this is a bad idea – unless you melt it into caramel, when it is sublime.

VARIATIONS

Garlic Popcorn

My favourite cinema has garlic granules, salt and cayenne pepper set out on the counter for eaters to sprinkle on their popcorn as desired. At home I often toss in a chopped fresh garlic clove or two, or add some garlic to a little butter and pour it over the hot popcorn.

Cajun Popcorn

1 tablespoon each of fresh oregano
leaves and garlic granules
2 teaspoons paprika
1 teaspoon each of ground cumin,
cayenne pepper, dried thyme and
onion powder
½ teaspoon black pepper

◆ Sprinkle the above Cajun spice mixture over buttered or unbuttered
popped corn. Any leftover spice mix can be used to coat fish, burgers,
chicken, etc.

Chocolate-Hazelnut Popcorn

Bits of hazelnuts in a chocolatey caramel cloak this sweet popcorn. Serve the
chunks on a plate for everyone to help themselves.

vegetable oil
90–125g (3–4oz) popcorn kernels
90g/3oz hazelnuts
250g/8oz soft light brown sugar
90g/3oz golden syrup
125g/4oz butter
¼ teaspoon salt
3 heaped tablespoons cocoa powder
½ tablespoon bicarbonate of soda

◆ Put a tiny amount of vegetable oil in a deep, heavy saucepan, add the
corn kernels, and pop, as described on page 15. Tip the popcorn into
a large bowl.

◆ Place the hazelnuts in a heavy, ungreased frying pan and heat, shaking every so often, until they are lightly toasted and flecked with brown.
Remove from the heat. If they are not peeled, tip them into a clean
towel and rub them until their skins are removed. Discard the skins
and coarsely cut up about half the hazelnuts, leaving the rest whole.
Mix with the popcorn and tip on to one large or several smaller baking sheets.

◆ In a heavy saucepan, combine the brown sugar with the golden syrup,
butter, salt and cocoa. Bring to the boil over a medium-low heat and
continue boiling for 5–7 minutes or until a few drops of the syrup form
a ball when dropped into a glass of cold water.

- Remove the syrup from the heat and add the bicarbonate of soda. Take care because the mixture will foam up. Quickly pour this foaming mixture over the popcorn and nuts, tossing it all together with a wooden spoon to coat well. The caramel syrup will be very very hot at first, but it will cool quickly as you mix it with the popcorn.

- Cover the coated popcorn with a paper towel and leave in a dry place. Break it into small, bite-sized pieces when ready to serve.

Lucky Dips

Dips are fun, we all enjoy them: tangy, creamy or spicy, there is something about a dip that spells P-A-R-T-Y. It's easy to make your own and not only will they save you money, but they will be delicious too. Everyone will be so happy dipping and munching, the party will be all the more lively. The following three recipes can be served together, or individually. Together, they are easily enough to serve six.

Spinach Dip

This is a typical California-style party dip, and one that I doted on as a teenager. I still like it. Serve it with tiny boiled new potatoes, carrot and cucumber sticks, and, okay, a few potato crisps, for dipping. When fresh spinach is not available at a good price, use frozen.

250g/8oz cooked spinach, finely chopped
3 spring onions, chopped
3 cloves garlic, chopped
1 tablespoon chopped fresh dill or ½–1 teaspoon dried dillweed, or to taste
¼ stock cube of choice dissolved in

about 1 tablespoon hot water (preferably cooking water)
175g/6oz mayonnaise
175g/6oz plain yogurt (either low-fat or Greek)
½–1 teaspoon lemon juice
salt and pepper

- Mix the spinach with the spring onions, garlic, dill, dissolved stock cube, mayonnaise and yogurt. Season with lemon juice, salt and pepper, and chill until ready to serve.

Spicy Peanut Butter Dip

Serve with raw vegetables such as carrot and celery sticks, thick slices of cucumber, strips of pepper, red or white cabbage wedges or chunks, and so forth, as a sort of dipping version of the classic Indonesian salad, gado-gado.

3 cloves garlic, finely chopped
2–3 teaspoons finely chopped fresh
  ginger
½–1 fresh green or red chilli, finely
  chopped, to taste
2–4 tablespoons sugar
250g/8oz crunchy peanut butter
1–2 tablespoons each of soy sauce,

sesame oil and lemon juice
60ml/2 floz water
2–3 tablespoons chopped fresh coriander, to taste
a dash of hot pepper seasoning, such as
  Encona hot pepper sauce or Tabasco
  (optional)

◆ Purée the garlic, ginger and chilli in a blender with the sugar, peanut butter, soy sauce, sesame oil and lemon juice. When well combined, thin with the water, then mix in the coriander. Taste, and add more of any of the flavouring ingredients, as required. Add hot pepper seasoning if desired.

Middle-Eastern Coriander–Parsley Dip

This green herby dip is not only marvellous for dipping into with raw vegetables, but you could also serve it with a plate of felafel balls alongside for a DIY felafel party, or spread it on to naan bread and eat it with shreds of barbecued lamb. Use tahini if you can find it; if not, use the more easily available hummus.

½ bunch fresh coriander
½ bunch fresh parsley
3–4 tablespoons fresh mint leaves
  (optional)
3–5 cloves garlic, chopped
175g/6oz tahini or hummus
about 1 tablespoon lemon juice, to taste

¼ teaspoon each of ground turmeric,
  ground coriander and curry powder
salt and black pepper
a dash of hot pepper seasoning, such as
  Encona hot pepper sauce or Tabasco,
  to taste

- Finely chop the coriander, parsley and, if using, the mint. Put in a blender or food processor with the garlic, tahini or hummus, lemon juice, turmeric, coriander and curry powder, and whirl together until smooth. Add salt, pepper and hot pepper seasoning to taste.

Deep-fried Leek 'Frizzles'

SERVES 6

Enjoy as a nibble, or as a garnish for other dishes. I like to serve these with 'burgers' as a twist on classic American onion rings.

4–6 leeks, washed and sliced
olive oil
sea salt, to taste

- Separate the leek slices somewhat, and dry with a clean tea-towel if necessary. Pour the olive oil into a frying pan to a depth of about 5–7.5cm/2–3in. Heat the oil until it begins to smoke, then add as many of the leek slices as will fit into the frying pan (probably about one-third). They will sizzle and frizzle and look a bit of a mess until they turn crispy brown at the edges; they will also shrink somewhat in size as they fry. Remove the leeks from the pan and drain on absorbent kitchen paper. Add a little more oil to the pan, let it heat, and fry a second batch of leeks. Continue until all the leeks are fried. Sprinkle with salt before serving.

SAVE VEGETABLE SCRAPS

Save every scrap of vegetables and their cooking water (the ends of carrots, cooking water from green beans, onion skins, and so forth). After several days, you will have enough for a very nice little vegetable stock, soup or flavouring for a sauce. Toss either the bits or the stock, when you have made it, into the freezer and wait until company comes.

Red Chilli and Oregano Chickpea Fritters

SERVES 6

These fritters are nutty-tasting, almost addictive, and unusual in that they are made from soaked and puréed but not boiled chickpeas. This gives them a completely different flavour and texture. They are also very easy to make, though the chickpeas need to be soaked overnight. You can purée the chickpeas while they are still slightly frozen.

350g/12oz dried chickpeas (about 500g/1lb once soaked)
2 eggs
350–500ml/12–16fl oz milk
175g/6oz self-raising flour
3 tablespoons paprika
½ teaspoon cumin seeds
4 cloves garlic, coarsely chopped

½–1 teaspoon salt
2–3 tablespoons chopped fresh parsley
⅛–¼ teaspoon bicarbonate of soda
½ teaspoon fresh oregano leaves
several pinches each of coarsely ground black pepper and crushed dried red chilli
olive oil for frying (see Note, below)

+ Soak the chickpeas overnight in enough cold water to cover. Drain well. (Alternatively, use 500g/1lb pre-soaked chickpeas.)

+ Purée the chickpeas in a food processor, then mix in the remaining ingredients, except the oil. You should have a thick batter. If it is too thin, add more flour; if too thick, add more milk.

+ Heat about 5cm/2in oil in a heavy frying pan or wok. When it is just smoking, add the batter in dollops of 2 tablespoons each, and cook until golden brown and crispy on the undersides. Turn the fritters over and cook the second sides. Remove from the pan, drain on absorbent kitchen paper, and keep hot while frying the remaining fritters. Serve hot.

Note
Use pure olive oil or a blend of three-quarters vegetable oil and a quarter extra virgin olive oil. There is no need to use 100 per cent extra virgin olive oil for frying.

Sunflower Seed Nibbles

These crisp sunflower seeds are great for nibbling on: crunchy, savoury, and light enough to nibble the evening away. They are also cheap: a 100g/3½oz bag costs practically nothing.

100g/3½oz shelled sunflower seeds
½–1 teaspoon vegetable oil

½ teaspoon salt
a few shakes of soy sauce

◆ In a heavy frying pan, toss the seeds with the vegetable oil and salt, then heat and cook over a medium-high heat for about 6 minutes or until the seeds are lightly golden, turning every so often to prevent burning. Remove from the heat and shake in the soy sauce, then return to the heat and continue cooking and turning for a minute or two longer, or until the seeds are golden brown in spots and very toasted. Remove from the heat and place in a bowl. Serve as required.

Mexican-style Crisp-roasted Pumpkin Seeds

This is something delicious to do with the seeds you discard from a pumpkin, but if you do not have a pumpkin, you can purchase pumpkin seeds in their shells and prepare them this way to make them deliciously brittle-crisp.

◆ Carefully separate the pumpkin seeds from their stringy fibres. Rinse the seeds well, then place them in a bowl and cover them with generously salted water. Leave to soak for at least 1 hour.

◆ Drain the seeds and toss with a few teaspoons of vegetable oil and a few generous shakes of soy sauce. Spread in a single layer on a baking sheet or in a shallow baking tin and bake in the oven at 190°C/375°F/Gas Mark 5 for 30–40 minutes or until they are crisp and lightly browned, turning occasionally. If the seeds are cooking too quickly, lower the heat to 180°C/350°F/Gas Mark 4 or roast them for a shorter time. The shells should be so crunchy they break apart in your teeth, and they should be light enough to eat whole, shell and all.

Pacific Wave Cocktail

SERVES 1

250ml/8fl oz pineapple juice
1 measure of tequila
1–2 ice cubes
a sprig of fresh mint

• Pour the pineapple juice and tequila over the ice cubes in a tall glass. Garnish with the mint sprig.

Sex on the Beach Cocktail

SERVES 1

175ml/6fl oz cranberry juice
1 measure peach schnapps
1 measure vodka
1–2 ice cubes
a wedge of lime

• Pour the cranberry juice, peach schnapps and vodka over the ice cubes in a tall glass. Garnish with the wedge of lime.

MAKE SAVINGS ON DRINKS

Prepare ahead. Buy bottled water, wine or non-alcoholic drinks when they are on special offer. Keep them on hand until needed to reduce your entertaining costs.

Fruit Frenzy

SERVES 2

Frozen fruit smoothies are refreshing and healthy, and they make a lively addition to any brunch or informal snacky gathering. Add a shot of alcohol and they are even livelier!

1 piece of fruit, cut into bite-sized chunks, or a handful of berries and ½ piece
of fruit
250ml/8fl oz fruit juice
several ice cubes
sugar or honey, to taste
a dash of vanilla essence/flavouring

◆ Put all of the ingredients in a blender, cover and whirl until it forms a thickish icy mixture. Pour into two glasses and eat/drink right away.

Strawberry Blossom Smoothie

SERVES 2

350ml/12fl oz orange juice
175–250g/6–8oz strawberries, fresh or frozen
1–2 tablespoons honey or sugar
a dash of orange flower water (see Note, below)
a few ice cubes if using fresh, unfrozen berries

◆ Combine all the ingredients in a blender and whirl until thickened and icy. Serve straight away.

Note
Orange flower water is usually cheaper at Indian and ethnic shops than at supermarkets.

Antipasti, Meze, Tapas and Appetizers

2

Antipasti, Meze, Tapas and Appetizers

...nibble at a cocktail
party, or enjoy as a
starter with a selection
of the delicacies gathered
together on your plate...

Antipasti, Meze, Tapas and Appetizers

ANTIPASTI, meze and tapas are little things that you can pick up with your fingers and nibble at a cocktail party, or enjoy as a starter with a selection of the delicacies gathered together on your plate.

It is no accident that throughout the sociable regions of the Mediterranean, where life seems to revolve around the table, tapas, antipasti and meze have a life of their own. They might comprise of a selection of cold vegetables, relish-like salads, marinated olives or vegetables, or one central dish, such as roasted feta cheese, which everyone digs into with crusty bread, or tidy little morsels such as wedges of roasted vegetable pizza or broccoli tostadas.

Sometimes they are mere nibbles brought to you with drinks. At other times an entire meal can be made of tiny portions, perfect for lingering socializing.

This chapter contains a selection of very good little appetite-enticers, whether you begin your meal with them, or whether they *are* the whole meal.

Italian Sweet and Sour Pumpkin

SERVES 6 as part of an appetizer

The sweet, spicy, tangy sauce with plump raisins is like a spicy caponata, and is marvellous as part of an antipasto or Mediterranean meze. For added texture, I sometimes sprinkle with toasted slivered almonds or pinenuts.

3 tablespoons extra virgin olive oil
500g/1lb pumpkin, peeled, deseeded
   and cut into 5mm/¼in slices
pinch of sugar
⅛ teaspoon each of ground cinnamon
   and allspice, or to taste
2 cloves garlic, chopped
400g/14oz canned chopped tomatoes
   (with their juice), or 400g (14oz) fresh
   tomatoes, diced, and 125ml/4fl oz
   tomato juice or passata

2–3 tablespoons raisins or sultanas
1 tablespoon sugar
½ teaspoon paprika
2 tablespoons red wine vinegar
salt and cayenne pepper or crushed
   dried red chilli, to taste

◆ Heat 2 tablespoons olive oil in a large frying pan and lightly brown the sliced, peeled pumpkin, sprinkling with the pinch of sugar, the cinnamon and allspice towards the end of the browning. You will probably need to do this in batches. Remove the pumpkin to a plate.

◆ Pour the remaining oil into the hot pan and add the garlic. Cook for a moment or two until fragrant but not brown. Quickly add the tomatoes, raisins or sultanas, 1 tablespoon sugar, the paprika and vinegar, and simmer for a few minutes to reduce the tomatoes to a thick sauce. Return the pumpkin to the pan, season with salt and cayenne or crushed dried chilli and adjust the sugar and vinegar content, if necessary. Serve warm or leave to cool and serve at room temperature.

Note
Don't waste the seeds from inside the pumpkin; use them to make Mexican-style Crisp-roasted Pumpkin Seeds (page 21).

Grilled Cumin Aubergine with Rouille

SERVES 6

The grilled aubergine is also good served with any raita or yogurt, or as a side dish alongside rice, pasta or couscous.

2 medium-large aubergines, sliced lengthways or crossways
salt for sprinkling
2 tablespoons extra virgin olive oil

For the rouille
1½ teaspoons each of paprika and mild chilli powder
¼ teaspoon cumin seeds

1 clove garlic, chopped or crushed
1 tablespoon extra virgin olive oil
4 heaped tablespoons mayonnaise
2 teaspoons chopped fresh coriander
juice of ¼ lemon or lime, or to taste
salt
hot pepper seasoning, such as Encona hot pepper sauce or Tabasco (if needed)

◆ Sprinkle the aubergine slices generously with salt, then leave for at least 30 minutes and up to 1½ hours. They will disgorge a certain amount of brownish liquid. Rinse them well, then pat them dry with absorbent kitchen paper. Brush both sides of the aubergine slices with olive oil, and arrange them on a baking sheet.

◆ Meanwhile, make the rouille. Combine the paprika, chilli powder and cumin seeds with the garlic and olive oil, then stir this mixture into the mayonnaise. When it is well combined, add the coriander and lemon or lime juice. Taste for seasoning and add salt and/or hot pepper seasoning, as needed. Chill until ready to serve; as it chills it will firm up.

◆ Grill the aubergine slices until they are lightly browned on one side, then turn them over and repeat on the second side. They should be lightly browned on the outside and tender within. Serve hot or at room temperature, with a bowl of the rouille for dipping or spreading.

Garlicky Feta Cheese and Fresh Herbs Wrapped in Pitta

SERVES 6

Inspired by the Persian classic dish of fresh herbs and flat bread, sabzi 'kordan', this simply prepared appetizer is utterly enticing: a cloth-wrapped pile of warm, soft pitta or naan breads, a bowl of tangy garlicky feta cheese and a plate of fresh herbs and raw salad vegetables. Each eater takes a piece of pitta, spreads it with the cheese and piles on herbs and vegetables. This little sandwich is then rolled up and nibbled, with a glass of red wine alongside.

250–300g/8–10oz feta cheese
3–4 cloves garlic, chopped
2 tablespoons olive oil
2–3 tablespoons plain yogurt
4 spring onions, trimmed and cut lengthways into halves or quarters

a little pile each of fresh dill, tarragon, coriander and mint
½ cucumber, cut into small sticks
1 small bunch radishes, trimmed
6 pitta or 3–4 naan breads

- Mash the feta cheese with a fork and add the garlic, olive oil and yogurt. Set aside.

- Arrange the spring onions, dill, tarragon, coriander, mint, cucumber and radishes on a plate. Set aside.

- When ready to serve, warm the pitta or naan breads. This can be done either in a heavy frying pan or a microwave. To cook in the pan, sprinkle each pitta with a few drops of water and warm them one at a time in a lightly oiled pan over a medium-high heat. To microwave, simply place them all on a plate, sprinkle with a few drops of water, and set the timer for about 60 seconds.

- When the breads are warm, stack them on a clean cloth-lined plate, and wrap them loosely in the cloth. Let each person break off bits of the bread and make his or her own little 'sandwiches' of cheese, herbs and salad.

Moroccan Carrot Salad

SERVES 6 as an appetizer

Carrot salads and relishes delight me. While I always expect to find the bright colour of carrots in northern European fare, often in rich or creamy dishes, I always find it a delicious surprise cooked with zesty spices, tangy lemon, pungent garlic and fragrant olive oil. Carrots are not only reliably cheap, but I find British carrots the best I have ever eaten: sweet, tender and earthy.

1.1kg/2¼lb carrots, sliced
pinch of sugar
3–5 cloves garlic, chopped
pinch of salt
½–1 teaspoon ground cumin or cumin seeds

1 tablespoon lemon juice or balsamic or raspberry vinegar, or to taste
3–5 tablespoons chopped fresh coriander
3 tablespoons olive oil (preferably extra virgin)

♦ Cook the carrots with the sugar, in boiling water to cover, for 5–10 minutes or until they are just tender and bright orange.

♦ While they are cooking, crush or combine the garlic with the salt, cumin, lemon juice or vinegar, coriander and olive oil.

♦ Drain the carrots and toss with the dressing. Enjoy warm or at room temperature.

Celeriac 'Salad' with Truffle

SERVES 6

A few drops of truffle oil is all it takes to transform humble celeriac, and a little bottle lasts and lasts. Nothing is quite so luxurious and memorable as being served a dish flavoured with truffle, and the few drops you drizzle on cost little. A good truffle oil, by the way, is really important; some of the cheaper oils just don't last and are less economical in the long run.

350g/12oz celeriac (about 1 small to medium root)
2–3 tablespoons extra virgin olive oil
1 teaspoon lemon juice, or to taste

1 clove garlic, finely chopped
salt and pepper
a few drops of truffle oil

- Peel the celeriac and cut it into slices. Cook the slices in boiling water for 6–8 minutes or until they are just tender. Drain, arrange the slices on a plate, and leave to cool slightly.

- Sprinkle the celeriac with olive oil, lemon juice, garlic, salt, pepper and, finally, a few drops of truffle oil. Serve at room temperature.

Grated Raw Swede with Raspberry Vinegar, Olive Oil and Capers

SERVES 6

This unusual salad is good as part of a selection of little salads as either French hors d'oeuvre, Italian antipasti, Mediterranean meze or the Moroccan kemia. It is based on the raw turnip salads I have enjoyed in Bulgaria; recently, when swedes were exceedingly cheap, I experimented with using them in place of the more usual small white turnip.

175g/6oz swede, peeled
1 tablespoon extra virgin olive oil, or to taste
1 teaspoon raspberry vinegar, or to taste
2–3 teaspoons capers (preferably

preserved in brine rather than vinegar), drained
1 teaspoon chopped fresh parsley, to serve (optional)

- Coarsely grate the swede. When ready to serve, toss the swede with the olive oil, vinegar and capers, mound on to a plate and sprinkle with parsley.

Fresh Cheese with Tomato-Ginger Chutney

SERVES 6

Inspired by the paneer chaat of India's Punjab, this dish consists of fresh cheese topped with a light and spicy salsa-like relish. The light, milky cheese contrasts delightfully with the fragrant, zesty chutney.

2 rounds of fresh mozzarella (about 125g/4oz each), cut into 2.5–5mm (⅛–¼in) slices, or other fresh cheese (see Variations, below)

Fresh Tomato–Ginger Chutney (see page 34)
fresh coriander or mint leaves to garnish (optional)

◆ Arrange the cheese on plates and, shortly before serving, spoon the relish around. Garnish if desired with coriander or mint leaves.

VARIATIONS

Any fresh cheese can be used in this simple dish, instead of traditional Indian paneer. Fresh mozzarella is easily available and reasonably priced, but Cypriot anari, Silican fresh Pecorino and Mexican queso fresco are all delicious; I've even prepared the dish for vegans using tofu. Greek feta can also be used but should be soaked in cold water for 1 hour beforehand to rid it of excess salt.

Crispy Indian Chickpea Fritters with Fresh Tomato-Ginger Chutney

SERVES 6

It's the contrast of rich and light, crisp and crunchy, fresh and tangy, that makes this appetizer of crisp spiced chickpea fritters tossed with fresh tomato chutney so special. Though it sounds complicated to prepare and strange to eat, it is actually the opposite: simple to make and intriguingly delicious.

350g/12oz chickpea (gram) flour
175ml/6fl oz water
3 tablespoons vegetable oil, plus more
   for frying
¼–½ teaspoon ground turmeric
3 cloves garlic, chopped
½–¾ teaspoon cumin seeds
¾–1 teaspoon salt

¼ teaspoon chilli powder or cayenne
   pepper (or more, to taste)
Fresh Tomato–Ginger Chutney (see page
   34)
extra chopped onions, chillies, coriander
   leaves and lime wedges to garnish
   (optional)

◆ Combine the chickpea flour, water, 3 tablespoons vegetable oil,
  turmeric, garlic, cumin, salt and chilli powder, and stir well until
  the mixture forms a paste-like batter. Leave to stand and thicken for
  20 minutes or so. Preheat the oven to 190°C/375°F/Gas Mark 5.

◆ Heat about 5cm (2in) oil in a large frying pan or wok. (A wok is best
  for this as it has a large surface area but uses relatively little oil.) When
  the oil is hot enough for frying (it should just smoke), place about half
  the batter into a large colander and force the mixture through the
  holes into the hot oil. Cook until the fritters are golden and crisp, then
  remove and fry the remaining batter. Drain the crisp fritters on
  absorbent kitchen paper, then place in a shallow layer in
  a baking tin. Bake in the oven for about 15 minutes or until they are
  sizzling and crisp. Leave to cool.

◆ Serve tossed with Fresh Tomato–Ginger Chutney, garnished if you like
  with a sprinkling of extra onions, chillies and coriander, and accompanied by lime wedges.

CHICKPEA FLOUR

When you have a bag of chickpea flour (known as 'gram' flour in Indian
groceries) on hand in the kitchen, you can make countless snack-like
dishes that cost hardly anything to throw together. It's a great trick to
have up your sleeve: beat chickpea flour with enough water and a little
bit of olive oil to form crêpes and you have the 'socca' of Nice; mix it
with spices and vegetables and you can fry it up into onion bhajis or
other vegetable pakoras.

Fresh Tomato–Ginger Chutney

SERVES 6

This zesty little relish is much like a Mexican salsa – fresh, invigorating and endlessly versatile – but with the fragrant whiff of fresh ginger to give it a distinctively Asian flavour. Like most Mexican salsas, this relish is free of fat, welcome to those who are counting calories or making room for a rich dessert. Make the chutney as mild or as hot as you like by varying the type and amount of chilli included.

1 onion, chopped
3 cloves garlic, chopped
2–3 teaspoons chopped fresh ginger
½ fresh green chilli, chopped (or more, to taste, depending on the heat of the chilli)
¼–½ teaspoon cumin seeds (or more, to taste)

2–3 teaspoons lemon juice
3–4 ripe fresh or canned tomatoes, finely chopped
60ml/2fl oz tomato juice (the juice from a can of tomatoes is fine)
3–4 tablespoons coarsely chopped fresh coriander
salt and black pepper

◆ Combine the onion, garlic, ginger, chilli, cumin seeds, lemon juice, tomatoes, tomato juice and coriander. Season to taste with salt and pepper.

Roasted Summer Vegetable and Pesto 'Pizza'

SERVES 6 as a starter; about 10 as part of a larger multi-coloured antipasto

These little 'pizzettes' are not traditional Italian fare but make a very delicious and exciting dish to start a meal. The roasted vegetables and pesto spell luxury, but if the vegetables are all in glorious and cheap peak of season, they'll cost pennies. Unfortunately, bottled pesto can be expensive, but you can use the remains of the jar during the following week. Alternatively, make a small batch of your own using fresh basil, and if your market sells basil only at a prohibitive cost, grow your own. Most summers will give you enough sun in your window for at least one nice batch of pesto.

Using flour tortillas as a base for pizza is simple and quick, and reasonably priced. I often buy them when they are on offer and pop them into my freezer for whenever I need them.

1 red pepper

2 small to medium courgettes

about 24 cherry tomatoes

about 2 tablespoons extra virgin olive oil

salt and pepper

6 flour tortillas

6 tablespoons tomato paste

2–3 cloves garlic, chopped

3–5 tablespoons pesto

175–250g/6–8oz grated cheese, such
   as mozzarella or Cheddar

3 tablespoons freshly grated Parmesan
   cheese

- Roast or grill the red pepper, turning it for even cooking, until it chars and blackens in spots. Remove from the heat and place in a plastic bag or pan with a tight-fitting lid. Leave to stand while you prepare and cook the courgettes and cherry tomatoes.

- Slice the courgettes lengthways about 5mm/¼in thick. Cut the cherry tomatoes into halves. Arrange the courgettes and tomato halves in the grill pan and brush or drizzle with olive oil. Grill until they are just tender but still somewhat crisp, brushing or drizzling with more oil as they cook. Sprinkle with salt and cut them into small dice. Set aside.

- Peel the pepper, discard the stem and seeds, and cut the pepper into slices.

- Arrange the tortillas on several baking sheets so that each tortilla is a flat uncovered surface. Spread them with tomato paste and sprinkle with garlic. Top with the diced courgettes and tomatoes, and the pepper slices. Dot with the pesto, then sprinkle with first the mozzarella or Cheddar and then the Parmesan. Drizzle with the remaining olive oil and grill each one for 5–8 minutes or until the cheese is melted and sizzling. Eat straight away.

Broccoli Tostadas with Parsley–Tomato Salsa

SERVES 6 as a starter; 10–12 cut into wedges as part of a selection of appetizers

One day not long ago I had a large amount of parsley languishing in the refrigerator and used it for a Mexican salsa, instead of the more usual coriander. Spooned on to broccoli tostadas, it complemented the spring-like flavour of the broccoli. You can use either maize or flour tortillas for this. Both are equally good, but flour tortillas are easiest to come by, and the maize tortillas available in Britain are often pre-fried or 'long-life'.

You will have extra salsa left over, but it will keep in the refrigerator for several days or you can freeze it in ice cube trays for later use.

For the salsa
3 cloves garlic, chopped
3 fresh green chillies, chopped (see Note, below)
400g/14oz can chopped tomatoes or fresh tomatoes, diced
salt, pepper and a pinch of sugar
½ teaspoon ground cumin (or more, to taste)
3–5 tablespoons chopped fresh parsley, or parsley and coriander mixed
1–3 tablespoons wine vinegar, to taste

For the tostadas
½–1 head of broccoli, cut into florets
6 flour tortillas
vegetable oil for brushing
250g/8oz grated sharp cheese, such as Cheddar

- Purée or crush the garlic with the chillies, then purée in a blender with the tomatoes (including the juice if using canned). Season with salt, pepper and sugar, then add the cumin, parsley, or parsley and coriander, and vinegar. Taste and adjust the seasoning, if necessary, and set aside.

- Steam the broccoli until it is *al dente* (tender but still slightly crisp), then remove from the heat and rinse with cold water to stop further cooking. Set aside.

- Arrange the tortillas on flat baking sheets and brush lightly with oil. Grill each one for 3–4 minutes until just slightly crisp and golden on one side. Turn the tortillas over and sprinkle the uncrisped side of each one generously with cheese, then scatter with florets of broccoli and dabs of salsa, as desired. Return to the grill and cook until the cheese melts and sizzles, then serve straight away, with extra salsa if desired.

Note

You may or may not remove the seeds from the chillies. Many people claim that the seeds are the hottest part but, from experience, I believe this to be untrue. It is the stringy membranes that cling to the inside flesh of the chilli and hold the seeds in place that can be so very, very hot. The seeds themselves have a nutty, though also hot, flavour. Removing the seeds cools the chilli down somewhat because these membranes are removed with them. In Mexico, the seeds will sometimes be kept and added to another recipe for the slightly nutty flavour they contribute.

Goats' Cheese Quesadillas

SERVES 6

The combination of tangy goats' cheese and rich melted Cheddar is seductive, all wrapped up in a tender flour tortilla with just enough chilli to make your mouth feel like dancing! This is a great starter as it is, or serve it in tiny bites for parties.

6 flour or high quality corn tortillas
2–3 rounds (60–100g/2–3½oz) goats'
  or feta cheese, crumbled
3 cloves garlic, chopped

250g/8oz Cheddar cheese, grated
Tabasco sauce, to taste
3 tablespoons chopped fresh coriander
vegetable oil for frying

◆ Following the directions on the packet, heat the tortillas one at a time in the microwave or a heavy, non-stick frying pan to make them pliable. Sprinkle the warm, pliable tortillas with the goats' or feta cheese, garlic, Cheddar, Tabasco and coriander, then fold over and press to seal well.

◆ Heat the filled tortillas in a non-stick frying pan with a few drops of oil, turning them once or twice, until they are lightly browned, and the cheese has melted. Alternatively, heat the tortillas in the microwave. Serve hot, with extra Tabasco and/or coriander on the side.

Goats' Cheese Crostini with Beetroot 'Caviar'

I whipped this festive appetizer up one night when I found myself with a crowd of eager people sitting at my table, looking towards me expectantly. In my kitchen I found stale bread (excellent for crostini), some goats' cheese I bought back from France, and pack of beetroot. The combination is superb.

300–350g/10–12oz bread, such as baguette cut on a slant, or slices of a rustic whole wheat loaf
about 6 tablespoons extra virgin olive oil
3 cloves garlic, chopped
6 cooked beetroot (about 500g/1lb), peeled
2 shallots or ½–1 onion, finely chopped
2 tablespoons red wine vinegar, or to taste

½ teaspoon sugar, or to taste
2 teaspoons chopped fresh dill or ½ teaspoon dried dillweed, or to taste
100g/3½oz goats' cheese (the kind with a rind)
salad leaves (including chopped spring onions and fresh dill), to garnish

◆ Preheat the oven to 180°C/350°F/Gas Mark 4. Brush the baguette or bread slices with about 2 tablespoons olive oil. Arrange on baking sheets and bake in the oven for 30 minutes or until lightly crisp and golden brown on both sides, turning once or twice. Remove from the oven and cut large slices into fingers. Sprinkle with the chopped garlic and leave to cool.

◆ Dice the beetroot and combine it with the shallots or onion, red wine vinegar, sugar, dill and the remaining olive oil. Taste for seasoning and adjust the ingredients, if necessary, for a good balance of sweet and sour.

◆ Slice the goats' cheese and spread or arrange on bread crostini. Grill until the cheese is warmed through and just slightly melted in places. It should sizzle slightly.

◆ Place some of the beetroot mixture in the centre of six plates, reserving any leftover dressing. Surround with crostini, and garnish with a few salad leaves tossed in the reserved dressing.

Peruvian Escabèche of Fresh Sardines

SERVES 6

Like the ceviche of the rest of Latin America, Peruvian escabèche involves pickling fish, but in this case the fish to be pickled is precooked, not raw as in Mexico. For a modest starter, serve the escabèche with a little lettuce; for a heartier dish or a summer lunch, accompany it with steamed or boiled potatoes, sweet potatoes and rounds of corn on the cob.

500g/1lb fresh or frozen sardines, cleaned
salt and black pepper
4 tablespoons flour
4–6 tablespoons extra virgin olive oil
2 carrots, thinly sliced
1 medium onion, thinly sliced
1–2 fresh green chillies, thinly sliced
125ml/4fl oz white wine vinegar

60ml/2fl oz water
juice of 1 lime
2 ripe tomatoes, diced
¼ teaspoon fresh oregano, or to taste
¼ teaspoon cumin seeds, or to taste
pinch of sugar (optional)
2 tablespoons chopped fresh coriander
hot chilli sauce, to taste

◆ Sprinkle the sardines with salt and pepper, then dredge them with flour and shake off the excess.

◆ Heat the oil in a heavy frying pan until it is just smoking. Add the fish, working in batches if you need to in order to avoid overcrowding the pan, and cook for 5–7 minutes on each side.

◆ Meanwhile, put the carrots, onion, chillies, vinegar and water in a saucepan, bring to the boil and cook for about 5 minutes.

◆ Remove the fish to a wide, shallow serving dish. Pour the vinegar into the pan with the vegetables and cook down until the vegetables are just tender and the vinegar reduced by about half. Pour over the fish and add the lime juice, tomatoes, oregano, cumin seeds, a tiny pinch of sugar and, if liked, the coriander. Taste and adjust the seasoning, adding hot chilli sauce to taste. Leave to cool, and enjoy at room temperature.

Punjabi-style Spinach

SERVES 6 as part of a selection of appetizers

Sag and palak are two types of spinach dish, both simmered with spices and often including other ingredients such as new potatoes (alu palak), tender lamb (sag gosht), chicken (sag murgh), spicy meatballs (sag keema), or firm Indian cheese (palak paneer).

This rendition is Punjabi, courtesy of our friend, Kashif Taj, an inspired cook who often rings his mother for recipes from her native Lahore, then cooks them up to share.

We like to serve this spinach dish untraditionally, as an appetizer, giving it a chance to shine in its own glory. It is delicious spread on to little pieces of bread, pitta or naan, or triangles of chappatti.

2 large onions, thinly sliced
2–3 tablespoons butter, or butter and vegetable oil
5–6 cloves garlic, chopped
1½–2 teaspoons chopped fresh ginger
2–3 fresh medium-large tomatoes, diced
1 teaspoon each of garam masala, paprika and salt
¼ teaspoon each of black pepper and cayenne pepper, or to taste
2–3 small fresh green chillies, chopped
2 bay leaves

7.5–10cm/3–4in fresh lemon grass, lightly crushed or thinly sliced
4–5 cardamom pods
1.1kg/2¼lb fresh spinach, trimmed of stems and cut into small pieces
1 small bunch fresh coriander (about 15g/½oz), coarsely chopped

To serve
4 pittas, 2 naans, 4 slices of white bread or 2 chappattis, cut into strips or triangles
250g/8oz plain yogurt

- Sauté the onions in the butter (or butter and oil) for about 10 minutes or until they are lightly golden and soft, then add the garlic and ginger and cook for a few moments. Add the tomatoes, garam masala, paprika, salt, black and cayenne pepper, chillies, bay leaves, lemon grass and a cardamom, and stew together for about 5 minutes or until the tomatoes are pulpy.

- Add the spinach, cover, and cook for about 20 minutes. Stir in the coriander, and serve warm or at room temperature, spread on to your chosen bread and accompanied by a dab or two of yogurt.

Anti-vampire Garlic–Pesto Bread

SERVES 6

Garlic-redolent bread, dripping buttery pesto juices, and crunchy from its cloak of crisp browned Parmesan cheese – delicious to munch on while the rest of the meal is roasting away over the coals.

I made this on Jane Asher's *Good Living* (BBC 1) not long ago, and was gratified to see our eaters – who might not otherwise have been too keen on garlic – munching this with unrestrained enthusiasm and glee.

2 baguettes (see Note, below)
15 cloves garlic
1 teaspoon salt, or to taste
125–185g/4–6oz unsalted butter,
    softened

125ml/4fl oz olive oil
up to 1 small jar pesto
185–200g/6–7oz Parmesan cheese,
    freshly grated

- Slice the baguettes lengthways, then score them into individual pieces without cutting right through. Crush or purée the garlic with the salt until it becomes a paste. Mix this with the softened butter, then work in the olive oil and as much pesto as you like (I would use the entire jar). Mix in the Parmesan cheese.

- Spread this buttery pesto mixture on the baguettes, taking care to get right to the edges and also into the scored crevices that separate the slices.

- Preheat the oven to 190°C/375°F/Gas Mark 5, or light the barbecue. Lay the open baguette lengths on foil or a baking sheet, cut and spread sides up, then cook on the barbecue or in the oven until lightly browned and crispy edged. Eat straight away.

Note
Use slightly stale bread for this – a saving in money, and equally delicious to eat.

Opposite page 40: Garlic Mussels with Rouille (page 43)
Opposite: Mixed Ravioli with Spring Vegetables (page 76)

Celeriac and Potato Tarte Tatin with Fresh Tarragon and Tomato–Mustard Vinaigrette

SERVES 6 as an appetizer or accompaniment to roast chicken

This little savoury tarte Tatin is very 'bistro'. Though the surrounding tomato–mustard vinaigrette or salsa is delicious, and quite attractive drizzled on to the plate to garnish the tart, it is optional and can be omitted if you'd like to serve the tart cut into wedges (or prepared as tiny individual tarts) alongside a roast chicken, with the defatted pan juices drizzled over both.

175–200g/6–7oz each of peeled celeriac and potatoes
30g/1oz butter
1 leek, white part only, or 3–4 shallots, chopped
salt and pepper
1–2 cloves garlic, chopped
1 teaspoon chopped fresh tarragon
a few drops of lemon juice
300–350g/10–12oz puff pastry (thawed if frozen)

a few sprigs of fresh tarragon to garnish (optional)

For the vinaigrette/salsa
400g/14oz can chopped tomatoes, or fresh tomatoes, diced
1–2 cloves garlic, chopped
1–2 teaspoons whole grain mustard
1 teaspoon white wine vinegar
3 tablespoons olive oil
2–3 teaspoons chopped fresh tarragon

- Thinly slice the celeriac and potatoes. Heat the butter until it is foaming, then add the celeriac and potatoes, and cook quickly for about 5 minutes, until they are golden but not cooked through. Add the leek or shallots and cook for a few more minutes. Season with salt and pepper and add the garlic, chopped tarragon and lemon juice.

- Preheat the oven to 190°C/375°F/Gas Mark 5. Roll out the pastry thinly to fit a 30cm/12in pie dish, allowing an extra 5cm/2in all round. Arrange the celeriac and potatoes evenly in the bottom of the pie dish, then top with the pastry, allowing the extra to hang over the sides. Trim the sides evenly to the edge of the dish, then roll the edges inwards so that the pastry has a sort of border and covers the vegetables, but doesn't go up the sides of the pan.

- Bake the tarte in the oven for about 30 minutes or until the pastry is golden brown and the vegetables tender and creamily cooked through. Meanwhile, to make the vinaigrette/salsa, combine all the ingredients.

- Invert the pie on to a plate. Any pieces of potato or celeriac that cling to the bottom of the pan – and they will – can be plucked off and arranged on the vegetable layer of the tarte Tatin. Serve the tarte on a plate or cut into wedges, garnished with tarragon sprigs, if liked, and with a drizzling of the tomato–mustard vinaigrette/salsa.

Garlic Mussels with Rouille

SERVES 4 as a starter; 6–8 as an hors d'oeuvre or antipasto

Mussels are one of those delicacies that seem like they should cost more than they really do. They are delicious cooked on the barbecue and served with any spicy salsa, and equally delicious served with the spicy Provençal sauce, rouille.

5 cloves garlic, chopped
3 tablespoons olive oil
1.1kg/2¼lb mussels in their shells, scrubbed and beards removed
60–90ml/2–3fl oz dry white wine or fish stock

5–6 tablespoons finely chopped fresh coriander
juice of ½ lemon
double quantity rouille (page 28)

- In a large, heavy saucepan or sauté pan, heat the garlic in the olive oil just until it smells fragrant, then add the mussels and stir them around for a moment or two in the hot garlicky oil. Pour in the white wine or fish stock, cover, and cook over a medium heat for about 10 minutes or until the mussel shells pop open. Discard any mussels whose shells are still shut, then stir in the coriander and lemon juice.

- Serve the mussels in a bowl or on a platter, surrounding a bowl of rouille.

Tempura of Gingered Green Beans with Three Bright Dips

SERVES 6

The Japanese method of battering and deep-frying, called tempura, is marvellous – brittle-crisp batter-cloak on the outside, tender vegetables within. I like to give the dish an East–West, contemporary twist by featuring only one vegetable, such as the green beans in the recipe below. If they are not available, and spring onions are, they too are delicious and go well with the selection of dips on pages 17–18.

Having a rather non-conformist selection of three dips makes for sociable dipping and eating. If you like, make only one dip – each has a distinctive character. Leftover dips are quite useful in your next-day kitchen: add the Coriander and Red Chilli Dip (page 45) to a salad dressing or marinade; its overnight rest will tame the chillies somewhat. The Teriyaki Dip (page 45) also makes a great marinade, but is even better added to shredded cabbage and raw vegetables for a quickly tossed together Asian salad. The third salsa is unique – diced preserved lemons with chopped onions and tomatoes – and is easy and cheap if you have a jar of homemade preserved lemons (page 130) in your refrigerator. Any errant spoonfuls left over inevitably get tossed into the bowl of lightly olive-oiled pasta I have for my lunch the next day.

2 eggs, separated
1 teaspoon salt
750ml/24fl oz chilled or cold water
400–500g/14–16oz plain flour
1 teaspoon bicarbonate of soda
1 tablespoon grated or diced fresh
　ginger

500g/1lb green beans, such as Kenya,
　fine or dwarf beans
flour for dredging
vegetable oil for frying
selection of dips and salsas, to serve
　(see opposite)

- Lightly beat the egg yolks with half the salt and beat in the water, then add the flour, bicarbonate of soda and ginger. Set aside for a moment.

- Whisk the egg whites with the remaining salt until it forms peaks, then fold about a quarter of the yolk mixture into the whites, then fold that mixture back into the rest of the yolk mixture.

- Top and tail the green beans, rinse in cold water, then shake them dry. Dredge them in flour, shake off the excess, then place them in the batter and coat them well.

- Pour oil to a depth of about 5cm (2in) into a heavy frying pan, and heat until it is just smoking. Add some of the battered green beans, taking care that you have a tempura of individual beans with a few clusters, rather than too much batter, which would make heavy green bean pancakes instead. You will probably need to work in several batches.

- Fry the beans until they are golden brown on one side, then turn them over and cook until golden brown on the second side. Remove and place on absorbent kitchen paper, then transfer to a baking sheet and keep warm in a low to medium oven until the last batch is fried. Serve straight away, hot and crisp, with a selection of dipping sauces and salsas.

Teriyaki Dip

4 tablespoons dark soy sauce

1 tablespoon sugar

1 clove garlic, chopped

1 teaspoon chopped fresh ginger

- Combine the soy sauce with the sugar, garlic and ginger. Leave to stand until ready to serve.

Coriander and Red Chilli Dip

125ml/4fl oz white wine vinegar or rice vinegar and lemon juice mixed

2 teaspoons crushed red chillies

2 cloves garlic, chopped

¼–½ teaspoon cumin seeds

salt

3 tablespoons chopped fresh coriander

- Heat the vinegar, or vinegar and lemon juice, until it just forms bubbles around the edge. Pour it into a bowl and add the chilli, garlic, cumin and salt. Leave to cool, then stir in the coriander.

Tomato and Preserved Lemon Salsa

3–4 ripe tomatoes
½ preserved lemon (or more to taste),
   see page 130

½ white onion or 2 spring onions,
   chopped
2 tablespoons liquid from the preserved
   lemon

* Dice the tomatoes and place them in a bowl. Dice the preserved lemon and add to the tomatoes with the onion and preserved lemon liquid. If the mixture is too chunky and not liquid enough, add a little fresh lemon juice.

Oeufs en Meurette with Rosemary Crostini

SERVES 6

Simply boiling down red wine with a wisp of aromatics and a little stock gives you the classic 'sauce meurette'. Served over poached eggs, it is a bistro classic and an extremely economical and impressive starter. A bottle of simple red wine, costing no more than a few pounds, will do to gild the humble, inexpensive egg. Whenever I serve Oeufs en Meurette, my guests say things like, 'Why don't I think of eating eggs more often?' And while this dish is sublime prepared with carefully reared organic free-range eggs, the truth is that I've made it with very cheap super-market eggs and it was also terrific. Serve one or two poached eggs for this. I serve one at home, but in Parisian bistros the plates usually contain two delectable eggs. As always, take the usual precautions: don't eat softly cooked eggs if you are pregnant, very young or very old, or are immunologically suppressed.

The rosemary crostini are my personal adaptation – delicious with the wine sauce and delicate eggs – and if you use leftover bread, along with garden rosemary, it's practically free.

1 baguette (preferably stale), sliced diagonally

1–2 tablespoons olive oil, or melted butter mixed with a little vegetable oil

7 cloves garlic, coarsely chopped

2 tablespoons chopped fresh rosemary

1 bottle red wine of choice (a Bulgarian merlot or country red is fine)

½ onion or 5 shallots, chopped

½ carrot, chopped

several sprigs fresh thyme and rosemary

1–2 bay leaves

½ stock cube (vegetable, chicken or beef)

250ml/8fl oz water

a few drops of red wine vinegar, or a few tablespoons of balsamic vinegar, plus extra for poaching the eggs

salt and pepper

15g (½oz) butter, softened

1 tablespoon flour

6 or 12 eggs, as desired

◆ Preheat the oven to 180°C/350°F/Gas Mark 4.

◆ To make the rosemary crostini, brush the bread with the oil, or butter and oil, and arrange on a baking sheet. Bake in the oven for 25–30 minutes or until the breads are golden and crunchy on both sides, turning once or twice. Finely chop together two cloves of the garlic and the chopped rosemary. Spread this over the crostini, rubbing it in, and set them aside.

◆ Pour the wine into a large saucepan and add the onion or shallots, carrot, remaining garlic, thyme, rosemary, bay leaves, stock cube and water. Bring to the boil, then reduce the heat and cook over a medium-high heat until the liquid has reduced to about a quarter. Season with a few drops of vinegar or balsamic vinegar, salt and pepper, then mix together the butter and flour and swirl it into the hot wine sauce. Cook for a few moments until it thickens, then remove from the heat and keep warm.

◆ Fill one or two deep frying pans with water, and heat until bubbling around the edges. Pour in a few tablespoons of vinegar. Slip one or two eggs at a time into a teacup or bowl, then slide them into the water. Cook the eggs for 3–4 minutes or until cooked to your liking. I like my poached eggs best when the whites are set and the yolk deliciously runny. Remove from the pan with a slotted spoon and place on a plate to dry off slightly.

◆ Heat the sauce, then place the egg(s) on individual plates and blanket them with the warm sauce. Serve straight away with the crostini.

Tortilla Andalucia

SERVES 6 as a starter or lunch dish; 12 as an appetizer

Chunks of this thick flat omelette, bursting with bits of tomato, lusty red peppers and rustic satisfying potato, are one of the most outstanding dishes you can serve your guests, a humble peasant dish that is irresistible and more-ish. I was first fed this tortilla by my 90-year-old olive grower host in Andalucia. The humble dish of potatoes, peppers and eggs was served in little squares, glistening with the olive oil it was cooked in; it far outshone the rarer, more costly foods that followed.

extra virgin olive oil for frying
6 large baking potatoes, peeled and
   diced
2 onions, chopped
10 cloves garlic, chopped
salt and coarsely ground black pepper
2–3 teaspoons chopped fresh rosemary
12 eggs, lightly beaten
2 red peppers, deseeded and thinly
   sliced or coarsely chopped

400g/14oz can chopped tomatoes or
   750g/1½lb fresh tomatoes, diced
pinch of sugar
½ teaspoon chopped fresh oregano or
   mixed Mediterranean herbs, such as
   herbes de Provence
handful of fresh basil leaves or parsley,
   coarsely chopped (optional)

◆ Heat 3 tablespoons olive oil in a large, heavy frying pan and add the potatoes, half the onions and half the garlic. Cover and cook over a medium-low heat for 15 minutes, turning every so often so that potatoes cook and turn golden rather than fry to a crisp brown. When the potatoes are just tender, remove to a large bowl and season generously with salt and pepper. Add the rosemary, a little more of the chopped raw garlic and about two-thirds of the beaten eggs. Set aside while you cook the peppers and tomatoes.

◆ Heat another 2 tablespoons oil in the same heavy frying pan and lightly sauté the remaining onion with half the remaining garlic for about 5 minutes or until the onion is softened. Add the peppers, cover and cook for a few minutes until the peppers soften, then add the tomatoes and sugar, season with salt and pepper, and cook over a high heat until the mixture has thickened and the liquid evaporated. Stir in the oregano and the remaining garlic, and taste for seasoning. Transfer the mixture to a bowl. Heat a few more tablespoons olive oil in the frying pan and, when it is hot, pour in the potato and onion mixture, smoothing it down so that it forms a flat pancake-like cake. Spread the peppers and tomatoes over this, forming a sort of lip around the edge of the circle of potatoes to keep in the next layer of eggs. Sprinkle with basil or parsley, if using, then pour on the remaining eggs. Cover and cook over a medium-low heat for about 10 minutes or until the egg mixture seems solid around the outer part of the circle and the bottom of the tortilla is golden brown. (Don't worry if the bottom is a *little* burnt (easily done) – it only adds to its rustic charm, and burnt patches can be trimmed off when you serve the tortilla.)

◆ Drizzle a little olive oil over the top of the tortilla and place it under the grill to firm up and lightly brown the top. Carefully loosen the edges of the tortilla with a knife and, when it has cooled somewhat, invert it on to a large plate or platter. If it falls apart, patch it up; it will hold together once it cools.

TURN TRIMMINGS INTO GARNISHES

Save little bits of things that would otherwise get thrown out and use them as a garnish or to enhance the flavour of another dish. The tops of peppers, for instance, if carefully removed and trimmed of their stems, can be chopped finely and sprinkled around the rim of a plate or on to a fruit salsa. A slice of two of cucumber taken from a salad can give you a lovely garnish of finely chopped cucumber for grilled fish or to add fresh crunch to an appetizer.

Soups

3

Soups

...thick and chunky,
smooth and silky,
hot or cold, soups
are a thrifty cook's
best friend...

Soups

WHETHER they are thick and chunky, smooth and silky, hot or cold, soups are a thrifty cook's best friend, providing ample scope for creativity with little bits of vegetables that would otherwise be thrown away. Think of the chef or home cook in France, where all sorts of bits and pieces get put aside for the evening potage. What could be more French than the evening soup of puréed winter vegetables, spring-time herbs, summer vegetables or autumn roots. Smooth and elegant, such soups are most likely enriched by last night's leftovers.

For many peasant cuisines, soup is a way of life: simmer the meat in a big pot of water and vegetables, and you have both a meat and a vegetable course in one, as well as the basis for soups and sauces in the days to come. Homemade peasant soups, hot or cold, are wonderful for entertaining – each brimming bowlful brings a sense of comfort and caring, and leaves your guests satisfied and content. The truth is that soup is easy, and it is thrifty, and it is marvellous.

Gazpacho

This is a classic version of a simple peasant soup, a liquid salsa, awash with olive oil and vinegar, and rich with the juices of the vegetables – a few foods are as reviving on a hot Mediterranean day.

Use a full-flavoured olive oil for this, and, believe it or not, canned tomatoes are fine. If, on the other hand, it is the fresh tomato season, then you should use fresh.

2–3 pieces stale, good quality country bread, broken into pieces
about 1 litre/32fl oz cold water
about 60ml/2fl oz extra virgin olive oil (preferably Spanish)
4 cloves garlic, finely chopped
1 green pepper, deseeded and finely chopped
1 cucumber, finely chopped
1 fresh red chilli (not too hot), thinly sliced

400g/14oz can chopped tomatoes, or 500–750g/1–1½lb fresh ripe tomatoes, diced, and 175ml/6fl oz tomato juice
1 teaspoon salt (or more, to taste)
¼ teaspoon ground cumin, or to taste
¼ teaspoon dried oregano, crumbled, or to taste
1 tablespoon sherry vinegar or red wine vinegar

◆ Moisten the bread with about 125ml/4fl oz cold water and a few tablespoons olive oil.

◆ Place the garlic, half the green pepper, half the cucumber, the chilli, half the tomatoes and all the tomato juice, if using, the soaked bread and 250ml/8fl oz water in a blender or food processor. Whirl until the vegetables are chopped and the mixture is thick and smooth. Add the salt, cumin, oregano, vinegar, a few more tablespoons olive oil and enough water to dilute the soup somewhat but not to create so much volume that it explodes out of the blender when you whirl it! Whirl again until it is smooth.

◆ Transfer the soup to a large jug and dilute it as required with more water. Add the remaining chopped vegetables and their juices. Taste for seasoning, and add salt, olive oil and vinegar to taste. Chill until ready to serve.

Sopa de Tortilla

SERVES 6

Sopa de tortilla is one of Mexico's favourite soups, a delicious combination of flavours and textures, with pieces of crisp corn tortilla added, like croûtons, to soak up the delicious broth. Of course if you were in Mexico, the quality of the tortilla chips would be something else: crisp and lightly salted, if salted at all, rather than blanketed with the false flavours you find in bagged chips over here. Real Mexican tortilla chips are the result of the frugal Mexican kitchen, for the tortillas they fry to a crisp are the slightly stale, already dry tortillas left over from the previous meal.

Good quality tortilla chips are usually sold under the description 'restaurant style' and can be costly. If you do happen to have corn tortillas lying around your kitchen – and no Mexican kitchen would be without them – cut them into wedges and fry the tortilla chips yourself. Don't bother if you only have flour tortillas, however; while they are marvellous for many things, they are no good for this dish.

A squirt of lime gives that refreshing tartness which so enhances spicy soups, and an optional dollop of sour cream or Greek yogurt is marvellous too.

1 onion, chopped
5 cloves garlic, chopped
2 tablespoons vegetable oil
1½ teaspoons each of paprika and mild
   chilli powder
½ teaspoon ground cumin
500g/1lb fresh tomatoes, diced, or
   400g/14oz can chopped tomatoes
1 carrot, sliced
1 courgette, yellow summer squash, or
   ¼ vegetable marrow, cut into bite-
   sized chunks
¼ cabbage, shredded or roughly cut up
½ green pepper, deseeded and diced,

and/or a handful of green beans or
   green runner beans, cut into bite-sized
   lengths
1.5 litres/2½ pints vegetable stock
¼–½ fresh chilli, chopped or thinly
   sliced
several large pinches of dried oregano
about 350g/12oz corn tortilla chips
3–5 tablespoons chopped fresh coriander
1 lime, cut into 6 wedges
sour cream of Greek yogurt to garnish
   (optional)

◆ Sauté the onion and half the garlic in the oil for 5–8 minutes or until the onion is softened, then stir in the paprika, chilli powder and cumin, and cook for 1–2 minutes to mellow out the spices. Stir in the tomatoes (with their juices if using canned), carrot, courgette or other squash, cabbage, green pepper and/or green beans, and stock. Bring to the boil, then reduce the heat and simmer over a medium heat until the vegetables are tender, that is verging on soft rather than fashionably *al dente*.

◆ Stir in the remaining garlic, along with the chilli and oregano. Warm the soup through and serve ladled into bowls and garnished with a handful of tortilla chips and a sprinkling of coriander, with a wedge of lime alongside for each person to squeeze in. Add a dollop of sour cream or Greek yogurt, if liked.

Spicy Chilled Garlic Soup from Provence

SERVES 6

This simple spicy barley and tomato soup is inspired by a North African Jewish soup. I've chilled it to a gazpacho-like state – utterly 'delish' on a sultry summer day. High summer is the only time you will have an abundance of cheap ripe tomatoes, and it's the one time when this soup really, really refreshes.

750g/1½lb fresh tomatoes, diced
1 fresh green chilli, chopped, or to taste
2 tablespoons olive oil
10–15 cloves garlic, peeled but left whole

100–125g/3½–4oz barley
2 litres/3¾ pints vegetable or chicken stock
several pinches of chopped fresh thyme or herbes de Provence

◆ Sauté the tomatoes and green chilli in the olive oil in a large saucepan for 6–8 minutes or until they are softened, then add the garlic, barley, stock and herbs. Bring to the boil, then reduce the heat and simmer for 40 minutes or until the barley is tender. Taste for seasoning, then chill until ready to serve.

Purée of Cauliflower Soup with Tarragon

SERVES 6

This rich purée of cauliflower tastes of an autumn Parisian supper: a warming, delicious soup that is as soothing on your budget as it is on your palate.

2–3 stalks celery, chopped

1 onion, finely chopped

30g/1oz butter or 15g/½oz butter and 1 tablespoon vegetable oil

2 tablespoons flour

1 litre/32fl oz stock of choice

1 small to medium cauliflower, trimmed and cut into florets

350ml/12fl oz milk (semi-skimmed is fine)

salt and a tiny pinch each of black and cayenne pepper

freshly grated nutmeg

2 tablespoons chopped fresh tarragon or ½ teaspoon dried tarragon

- ◆ Sauté the celery and onion in the butter (or butter and oil) in a large saucepan for 5–7 minutes or until lightly coloured and softened, then sprinkle in the flour and stir together, cooking for 1–2 minutes or until the flavour cooks through, but without browning the flour. Remove from the heat and stir in the stock, then return to the heat and continue to stir and simmer for 7–8 minutes or until the mixture is thickened. (It can remain as lumpy as you like, since it will be puréed.)

- ◆ Add the cauliflower and bring the mixture to the boil, then reduce the heat, cover, and cook over a medium-low heat for about 20 minutes or until the cauliflower is tender.

- ◆ With a ladle or slotted spoon, remove about one-third of the cauliflower florets and set aside. Scoop as much of the solids out of the soup as will fill about half the blender jar. Add half the milk and purée until smooth, then pour back into the soup along with the rest of the milk and the reserved florets. Season with salt, black and cayenne pepper and nutmeg, add the dried tarragon, if using, and heat until bubbles just form around the edge of the pan. Serve sprinkled with a little fresh tarragon, if using.

Leah's Tuscan Soup-Stew of Broccoli and Chickpeas with Pasta

SERVES 6

This rustic soup of beans, pasta and broccoli can be either a first course or a main course depending on the rest of the meal. If you are not in the mood for chickpeas, use red kidney beans of pink pinto or borlotti beans instead.

1 onion, chopped
5 cloves garlic, coarsely chopped
1 carrot, diced
3 tablespoons olive oil
425g/15oz can cooked chickpeas, drained or 250g/8oz drained, cooked chickpeas
1 potato, peeled and diced
400g/14oz can tomatoes
½ teaspoon mixed chopped fresh Italian or Provençal herbs (or more, to taste)

1 litre/32fl oz vegetable stock
1 head broccoli, cut into florets, the stems removed, peeled and diced
250g/8oz shell-shaped (conchiglie) or other macaroni-like pasta
salt and pepper
Parmesan or similar cheese, for grating, as desired
extra olive oil to serve (optional)

- Lightly sauté the onion, garlic and carrot in the olive oil in a large saucepan for 5–10 minutes or until softened, then stir in the chickpeas and potato and cook together for a few minutes, stirring.

- Add the tomatoes, herbs and stock. Bring to the boil, then reduce the heat and cook together for about 20 minutes or until the potato is cooked through. Take out about a quarter of the mixture of chickpeas and potatoes and mash or purée them, then return them to the soup.

- Add the broccoli to the soup and continue to cook for another 5–10 minutes. Meanwhile, cook the pasta in rapidly boiling salted water until just tender. Taste the soup for seasoning and add salt, pepper and more herbs, if you like – the soup is best with a good strong herbal taste. Drain the pasta and stir it into the soup. Warm through, then ladle into bowls and serve with grated cheese and, if desired, an extra drizzle of olive oil.

Spicy Mexican Fish Soup

SERVES 6

This is real Mexican fisherman's fare, ladled up in seaside cantinas along both the Pacific and Caribbean coastlines, or cooked on the fishing trawlers from the day's catch. It also makes a great soup for entertaining.

For the best effect without spending too much, use fish that is in season, and garnish with one or two higher priced luxury items. A few prawns go a long way when you see them; choose the smallest, which are usually the least expensive. To cut corners, you could omit the avocado and reduce the amount of prawns and seafood by half. As long as you can see a little squid, prawn or mussel poking up somewhere in the pot, your soup will be deemed luxurious.

3 waxy (boiling) potatoes

2 medium onions, chopped

6 cloves garlic, chopped

2 tablespoons olive oil (preferably extra virgin)

350g/12oz diced tomatoes (canned are fine)

1 bay leaf

¼ teaspoon oregano

½ stalk celery, chopped

2 fish stock cubes

hot pepper seasoning, such as Encona hot pepper sauce or Tabasco, to taste

1 litre/32fl oz water

12 mussels in their shells, cleaned and trimmed of beards

2 squid, cleaned and thinly sliced (including the tentacles)

12 prawns, in their shells

250–300g/8–10oz fish fillet or steak, cut into bite-sized pieces

To serve

1 avocado

2–3 fresh green chillies, chopped

3 spring onions, thinly sliced

½ bunch fresh coriander, chopped

2 limes, cut into wedges

- Cook the potatoes in rapidly boiling salted water for about 15 minutes or until *al dente*. Remove from the heat, drain and leave to cool, then cut into bite-sized chunks or dice. Remove and discard the peel.

- Lightly sauté the onions and garlic in the olive oil in a large saucepan for about 5 minutes or until softened, then add the tomatoes, bay leaf, oregano, celery, stock cubes, a few shakes of hot pepper seasoning and the water. Bring to the boil, then reduce the heat and simmer for about 10 minutes or until the celery is no longer crunchy.

- Add the diced potatoes and mussels to the soup, and cook for about 5 minutes, then add the squid, prawns and fish. Simmer for a further 5–10 minutes or until the mussels have opened up and the squid, prawns and fish are opaque. Discard any mussels that have not opened. Ladle the soup into individual bowls to serve.

- Halve, stone, peel and dice the avocado and sprinkle over the soup with the chilli, spring onion and coriander. Garnish with wedges of lime.

ECONOMICAL COOKING

Being a good cook means being an economical one. Don't throw anything out! Save bits of vegetables to whirl into a puréed soup, like the French housewife does; chop stems from parsley, coriander and other herbs, then add them to your simmering stock; small amounts of meat, fish or poultry can be used as a garnish for salads, sandwiches, pasta or the following day's lunch for the cook; the wispy leaves of fennel make an excellent base for any French or Mediterranean fish soup.

Middle-Eastern Soup of Black-eyed Peas

SERVES 6

When my friend, a Sephardi from Israel, gave me this recipe years ago, her eyes lit up as she described the soup: 'You will like it,' she said. 'The little beans get very tender and the soup is hot and spicy.'

185g/6oz dried black-eyed peas
1– 1½ onions, chopped
6 cloves garlic, chopped
3 tablespoons extra virgin olive oil
1½ teaspoons each of ground cumin and turmeric
400g/14oz can chopped tomatoes

1.5 litres/2½ pints chicken or vegetable stock
60g/2oz (half a large bunch) fresh coriander, chopped
sea salt and cayenne pepper, to taste
2–3 tablespoons lemon juice

◆ Place the black-eyed peas in a saucepan with water to cover. Bring to the boil, then lower the heat and leave to stand for 2 hours. Drain, add fresh water to cover, and bring to the boil once again. Reduce the heat and simmer for 30–40 minutes, or until the peas are tender. Drain and set aside.

◆ Sauté the onions and garlic in the olive oil in a large saucepan for 5–10 minutes or until they are soft, then sprinkle in the cumin and turmeric, and add the tomatoes, stock, black-eyed peas and coriander. Return to the boil, then reduce the heat and simmer for 20–30 minutes. Taste and add salt and cayenne pepper. Add the lemon juice at the last minute, and serve hot.

MAKE THE MOST OF DRIED BEANS

Dried beans are cheap, versatile and exotic. Instead of thinking about entertaining menus starting with a great chunk of meat or packet of pasta, think about the satisfying spicy ethnic dishes that beans and legumes figure so prominently in. Any spicy meat stew can be stretched, Middle-Eastern style, by adding an equal amount of cooked beans/ legumes to the meat and vegetables.

Provençal Garlic Soup with Couscous or Pastina

SERVES 6

Garlic simmered in water or stock forms the basic of this classic Provençal soup, which can then be embellished in any one of several million ways. Sometimes the soup is austere – garlic and sage leaves boiled in hot water with a few crusts of stale bread to bulk it out; at other times it is rather more deluxe, as it is here, with its flavourful stock and enrichment of cheese. Parmesan cheese, by the way, is a most traditional French cooking cheese, going back centuries.

If you grow nasturtiums (and you should, for they add colourful festivity and a nippy watercress-like flavour to all they are scattered over, plus they are easy to grow), pick an assorted handful of brightly coloured blooms and cut them into fine strips. Scatter the confetti-like strands over the top of the soup just before serving.

15 cloves garlic
1.5 litres/2½ pints chicken or vegetable
  stock
large pinch of herbes de Provence, or
  several sprigs of fresh thyme, sage
  and rosemary

salt and cayenne pepper to taste
2–3 tablespoons olive oil.
90g/3oz couscous or tiny pastina such
  as acini di pepe
about 90g/3oz freshly grated Parmesan
  cheese

- Cut 10 of the garlic cloves into quarters or chunks and put in a saucepan with the stock and herbs. Bring to the boil, then reduce the heat and cook over a medium-low heat for about 10 minutes or until the garlic is softened.

- Meanwhile, crush the remaining garlic with a large pinch of salt. (Using a mortar and pestle brings out a stronger, more fragrant side to the garlic, releasing its aromatic oil to its fullest.) When the garlic becomes paste-like, stir in the olive oil and set aside.

- Stir the couscous or pastina into the hot simmering soup, and continue stirring for a few minutes so that it doesn't form lumps. Couscous will only take a few minutes to cook; pastina a little longer.

- Stir in the Parmesan cheese, then the garlic–olive oil mixture to taste, and serve straight away.

Salads

4

Salads

...starters or main
courses; crisp, raw and
crunchy or tender...
doused with a
vinaigrette or other
spritely dressing...

Salads

SALADS can be starters or main courses; crisp, raw and crunchy or tender cooked vegetables left to cool then doused with a vinaigrette or other spritely dressing. They can also contain nuggets of meat, poultry, fish or cheese, and they don't even need to be cold – think of the warm salads of France or South-east Asia. Make a summer salad lively and exotic by adding fresh fruit. Mangoes, grapes and peaches are perfect and invigorating.

Salad of Frisée Lettuce and Bacon

SERVES 6

This salad is one of the most memorable dishes you can serve, a classic of the bistro and as comforting as it is sophisticated. If frisée is beyond your budget for the moment, shredded cabbage, added to the pan and cooked for the last few minutes with the bacon, makes a very good substitute.

Garlic croûtons make a hearty, garlicky addition, and frugally use up any leftover bread you have languishing around the kitchen. If you are feeling a bit more ambitious, add a warm poached egg to each salad. As the egg is cut into, the runny yolk combines with the tangy dressing, and just might convince you that you are sitting at a paper-covered table somewhere near the Seine.

about 300g/10oz stale white country
    bread, thickly sliced
6 tablespoons extra virgin olive oil
3 cloves garlic, chopped
leaves of 1 large or 2 small frisée
    lettuces, washed, dried and cut into
    bite-sized pieces

2–3 shallots, chopped
250g/8oz bacon bits or bacon rashers,
    derinded and cut into pieces
3 tablespoons white or red wine vinegar

◆ Preheat the oven to 180°C/350°F/Gas Mark 4. To make the croûtons, cut the bread into large bite-sized pieces and place them on a baking sheet. Drizzle with 2 tablespoons of the olive oil and toss well. Bake in the oven for about 30 minutes, turning once or twice, or until the bread chunks are golden and crisp. Remove from the oven and toss them with the garlic. Set them aside while you prepare the salad.

◆ Toss the frisée with the shallots and the remaining olive oil, and set aside. Cook the bacon pieces in their own fat in a heavy frying pan, cooking slowly to extract nearly all the fat, then letting it crisp up as it fries.

◆ Pour off most of the fat, then spoon the bacon on to the salad. Pour the vinegar into the pan and heat over a high heat for a few moments until the mixture bubbles and reduces somewhat. Stir to mix any bacon bits into the hot vinegar, then pour it all over the salad. Toss well, add the croûtons, give it another toss, and serve straight away.

Pacific Rim Salad

SERVES 6 as a starter or light lunch

This unusual California-inspired salad combines Asian greens, mango and peanuts with warm grilled lamb, but any other meat, poultry or fish could be used instead of the lamb. If you've one or two portions left over from the night before's barbecue, you could use that. Similarly, ripe peaches or nectarines and/or kiwi, can be used in place of the mango.

400g/14oz mixed salad leaves, preferably containing mizuna
leaves of 1 round lettuce, cleaned and torn into bite-sized pieces
½ cucumber, cut into thin sticks
4 spring onions or shallots, thinly sliced
4 tablespoons chopped fresh coriander
3 tablespoons fresh mint or basil, thinly shredded or coarsely chopped
2–3 cloves garlic, chopped
250g/8oz lamb steak or chop
soy sauce to taste

3–4 tablespoons olive oil
½ teaspoon salt, or to taste
1 teaspoon sugar
½–1 teaspoon Tabasco sauce or crushed red chillies
1 tablespoon balsamic vinegar
2 limes
1 mango, peeled and cut from the stone into slices or bite-sized pieces
4–5 tablespoons coarsely chopped dry-roasted peanuts

♦ Combine the salad leaves with the round lettuce, the cucumber, spring onions or shallots, coriander, mint or basil and garlic. Leave in the refrigerator or in a cool place while you cook the meat.

♦ Pat the lamb dry on both sides, then cook over a high heat, either in a hot pan lightly rubbed with oil or on the barbecue, for 3–4 minutes on each side, until brown on both sides but still rare (slightly pink) inside. Remove from the heat and sprinkle with soy sauce to taste. Slice very thinly.

♦ Sprinkle the salad greens with the olive oil, salt, sugar, Tabasco or crushed chillies and balsamic vinegar, and toss well together. Cut one of the limes in half and the other into wedges. Squeeze the juice from the lime halves over the salad, then arrange the salad on individual plates or on one large platter. Arrange the meat and mango over the salad, sprinkle with the peanuts and serve with the lime wedges.

Hot Potato and Cheese Rosti on a Bed of Mixed Herb Salad

SERVES 6 as a starter or light lunch

Rosti is a crisp pancake of grated potatoes, creamy and earthy inside, unspeakably buttery on the outside. Served atop a bed of fresh crunchy salad leaves, it makes a delightful warm salad to serve as a starter or light main course. Half-boiling the potatoes before grating them stabilizes the starch so that they don't absorb so much fat. This is best done ahead of time – at least 2 hours and up to 3 days ahead.

5–6 medium to large potatoes
175–250g/6–8oz sharp cheese, such as Cheddar
salt and pepper
4–5 spring onions, thinly sliced
2–3 tablespoons vegetable oil or 30–45g/1–1½oz butter

several handfuls of mixed salad leaves
3 tablespoons chopped fresh parsley, chervil and tarragon (whatever is available)
3–4 tablespoons olive or walnut oil
1–2 tablespoons red wine vinegar

◆ Cook the potatoes in boiling salted water for about 10 minutes or until half tender but still crunchy. Drain and leave to cool.

◆ Grate the half-cooked potatoes, using the large holes of a grater. (I do not bother to peel the potatoes as much of the peel comes off in the grating and the rest just disappears into the potato mixture, giving it a nice earthy quality.) Grate the cheese using the same large holes, and toss with the potatoes, seasoning the mixture with salt and pepper, and adding the spring onions.

◆ Heat a non-stick frying pan and add the oil or butter. Place the potato and cheese mixture into it, forming one large pancake. Cook slowly over a medium-low heat until the bottom of the pancake is golden brown and crisp. Invert on to a plate, then slide back into the pan and cook the second side until it, too, is crisp and browned.

◆ Toss the mixed salad leaves with the fresh herbs and dress with the olive or walnut oil and the vinegar. Serve the hot pancakes cut into wedges and garnished with the vinaigrette-dressed salad leaves.

Hot and Sour Chicken Noodle Salad with South Pacific Flavours

SERVES 6 as a starter or light lunch

Spicy-sour flavours, a flash of chilli heat, the salty tang of soy, and the crunch of mixed salad leaves and peanuts, give this modern salad its pizzazz. The breasts of the chicken, or indeed a small piece of lamb cutlet, tender beef, or a handful of scallops or prawns can be used instead of chicken thighs if your budget allows and you prefer. Replace some or all of the cabbage with cucumber, cut into julienne, in spring, summer or autumn, or whenever it is reasonably priced.

300–350g/10–12oz boned chicken thighs, skinned if preferred

6 cloves garlic, chopped

juice of 3 limes or lemons

1 tablespoon olive or mild vegetable oil

2 dried red chillies, lightly crushed or broken up (about ½ teaspoon crushed chillies)

4 shallots, 1 onion or 4 spring onions, finely chopped

3 tablespoons fish sauce or light soy sauce

½ teaspoon sugar, or to taste

350g/12oz dried Chinese egg noodles

large handful each of fresh mint leaves and fresh coriander

½ white cabbage, coarsely chopped

3 tablespoons roasted salted peanuts

about 200g/7oz mixed salad leaves

- Combine the chicken thighs with half the garlic, 1 tablespoon lime or lemon juice, and the oil. Set aside for a few minutes while you prepare the rest of the ingredients.

- In a heavy ungreased frying pan, toast the chilli flakes over a medium heat until they smoke slightly. Remove from the heat, taking care not to inhale the pungent smoke. Combine with the remaining garlic, the shallots (or onion or spring onion), remaining lime or lemon juice, 2 tablespoons of the fish or soy sauce, and the sugar. Set aside.

- Cook the noodles according to packet instructions until they are just tender. Drain and rinse in cold water, then set aside to drain once again.

- Wipe the chicken pieces dry, then heat the frying pan and cook the meat quickly, searing it on each side, then reduce the heat and cook until the pieces are just cooked through (slightly firm to the touch). Remove from the heat and sprinkle with the remaining fish or soy sauce. Let it stand while you assemble the salad.

◆ Combine the noodles with the dressing, mint and coriander, add the cabbage. Lightly crush the peanuts, toss them in, then slice the chicken into strips and add it to the noodle mixture. Arrange the salad leaves on a platter or plates and pile the chicken noodle mixture on top. Serve at once.

Russian Potato Salad with Fresh Dill and Spring Onions

SERVES 6 as an appetizer or side dish

Given to me by an *émigré* from the former Soviet Republic, this potato salad is delicious alongside any barbecue, especially smoky grilled salmon, or serve it as part of a selection of appetizers, known as zakuski, for a buffet lunch or supper.

1.25kg/2½lb small new potatoes
5–8 spring onions, thinly sliced
3–4 tablespoons chopped fresh dill or about 1 teaspoon dried dillweed
3 cloves garlic, chopped
90–125g/3–4oz each of mayonnaise and Greek yogurt (or sour cream)

2–3 tablespoons capers, drained (optional)
juice of ½ lemon
salt and pepper
1 round lettuce, broken into leaves, or a handful of salad leaves, to serve

◆ Cook the potatoes by steaming or boiling until just tender, then drain well and allow to cool slightly. When cool enough to handle, cut them into chunks and lightly toss them with the spring onions, dill, garlic, mayonnaise, Greek yogurt or sour cream, capers and lemon juice. Add salt and pepper to taste. Chill, then serve on a bed of lettuce or salad leaves.

Pasta and Noodles

5
Pasta and Noodles

...elegant and rustic,
spicy or suave, chunky
or refined; basically,
pasta has it all...

Pasta and Noodles

PASTA, in all its forms, from pastina to spaghetti to lasagne to Chinese noodles, is the most perfect entertaining food I can think of, whether you are worried about your wallet or not. It comes in a dizzying variety of shapes and sizes – 734 last time I tried to count – and so versatile that whatever your garden has to offer will most likely be delicious with it. Ethnic flavours of nearly all persuasions are perfect with pasta, as is cross-cultural creativity.

Pasta is both elegant and rustic, spicy or suave, chunky or refined; basically, pasta has it all. And when you are watching your pennies, pasta is right there for your convenience and delight.

Fresh or dried, pasta takes only minutes to cook in lots of rapidly boiling salted water, but there are a few tips to remember:

- never overcrowd the pan;
- never add the pasta before the water boils;
- testing a piece is the best way to tell when it is cooked; it is *al dente* when it is just tender but still has some 'bite' (ie. some resistance 'to the teeth', hence the name *al dente*);
- don't stick rigidly to the cooking times given on packets; they are often too long.

Depending on portion size, pasta dishes can generally be either starters or main courses. Serving quantities for the following recipes are given for one or the other, or both, as appropriate.

Pasta Shells with Tomato, Bacon and Oregano

SERVES 6 as a starter; 4 as a main course

It's so deliciously savoury, you don't need grated cheese with this tomatoey bacon-studded pasta. The shell shapes trap splotches of sauce and bits of bacon in them, making each bite varied in taste and texture. Since bacon bits are deliciously salty and flavourful, you won't need the expense of cheese.

125–150g/4–5oz bacon bits or 4–5
   rashers lean bacon, derinded and cut
   into pieces
1 onion, chopped
3 cloves garlic, chopped
salt and black pepper
several pinches of sugar

2–3 tablespoons olive oil
2 × 400g/14oz cans chopped tomatoes
   or 1kg/2lb fresh tomatoes, diced, and
   250ml/8fl oz tomato juice or passata
½ teaspoon dried oregano leaves,
   crushed in your hands, or to taste
500g/1lb shell pasta (conchiglie)

- Lightly sauté the bacon pieces in their own fat in a non-stick frying pan with the onion for 5–10 minutes or until the onion is softened, then add the garlic and cook a few moments longer, sprinkling with salt, pepper and a little sugar as it cooks.

- If the bacon has rendered much fat, pour it off. Add the olive oil, stir the mixture around for a few moments, then add the tomato juice, if using fresh tomatoes, and cook over a high heat for about 7 minutes or until it is reduced to a thick paste-like mixture, then add the diced tomatoes and continue to cook for a further 8–10 minutes or until the mixture is thick and pulpy. If using canned tomatoes, add them with their juice and cook for 10–12 minutes or until thick and pulpy. Check the seasoning and stir in the oregano.

- Cook the pasta in boiling salted water until it is *al dente* (see page 72), then drain and toss with the sauce. Serve straight away.

Tagliatelle with Chicken Livers, Mushrooms and Broccoli

SERVES **6 as a starter; 4 as a main course**

Chicken livers, usually sold frozen in supermarkets, are a treat for the budget. If you are feeling very extravagant, I would try a drizzle of truffle oil over this, too, but if you feel the need to cut costs instead, forget the truffle oil and use spaghetti in place of the more elegant tagliatelle.

3–4 tablespoons extra virgin olive oil
grated zest of 1 lemon
125g/4oz chicken livers, washed, trimmed and cut into pieces between the size of a hazelnut and a walnut
1 onion, chopped
90g/3oz bacon bits, derinded
4 cloves garlic, chopped
1 head broccoli, cut into florets, the stems removed, peeled and diced
about 125g/4oz mushrooms, thinly sliced

salt and black pepper
125ml/4fl oz dry white wine or dry white vermouth
125ml/4fl oz chicken stock
400g/14oz can chopped tomatoes
pinch of sugar
6–8 fresh sage leaves, chopped
350g/12oz tagliatelle
50g/2oz Pecorino or other grana-type cheese, grated

- Heat 2 tablespoons of the olive oil in a frying pan and lightly fry the lemon zest, chicken livers, onion, bacon bits and three cloves of the garlic for 6–8 minutes or until the onion is softened and the chicken livers just cooked through. Remove to a plate or bowl.

- Add another tablespoon of oil to the pan and cook the broccoli and mushrooms, seasoning with salt and pepper, and sprinkling with garlic as they cook. Cook for only a minute or two, just enough for the broccoli to turn crisp-tender and bright green, and the mushrooms to lightly brown. Remove to the plate or bowl with the liver mixture.

- Pour the wine or vermouth into the frying pan and cook down, letting the wine soak up all of the juices from the livers, onion and vegetables. When the wine has reduced to a few tablespoons, add the stock and continue to boil for a few minutes more. Add the tomatoes, salt, pepper and a pinch of sugar, and cook for about 15 minutes, or until the sauce is richly reduced. Add the sage and the liver mixture, reduce the heat to very low and simmer while you cook the pasta.

♦ Cook the pasta in rapidly boiling salted water until it is *al dente*. Drain and toss with the sauce, then serve sprinkled with Pecorino.

Tagliatelle with Chorizo, Peas and Goats' Cheese Cream

SERVES **6 as a starter; 4 as a main course**

A tiny amount of chorizo adds a distinctive flavour to this sumptuous pasta dish.

1–2 medium onions, chopped
8 cloves garlic, chopped
3 tablespoons olive oil
100g/3½oz chorizo, thinly sliced
4–6 tablespoons tomato paste
185–250g/6–8oz shelled and blanched
 or frozen peas
170g/5½oz milk creamy goats' cheese,
 crumbled

up to 125ml/4fl oz milk
black pepper
500g/1lb tagliatelle
handful of fresh basil leaves, thinly
 shredded, or 1–2 teaspoons pesto
75–90g/2½–3oz Parmesan or Pecorino
 cheese, freshly grated

♦ Lightly sauté the onions and garlic in the olive oil in a saucepan for 5–10 minutes or until softened, then stir in the chorizo and cook for a few minutes with the onions. Stir in the tomato paste and peas, and cook through together for a few moments.

♦ Stir in the goats' cheese, then stir in just enough milk to smooth and thin the mixture to a thickish sauce consistency. Season with black pepper and set aside.

♦ Cook the pasta in rapidly boiling salted water until *al dente* (see page 72). Drain, but not well, leaving a small amount of hot water on the pasta. This will help to keep the sauce clinging to the pasta. Return the pasta to the saucepan with the sauce, and toss well together, then add the basil and grated cheese, and toss again. Heat through for a moment or two, then serve straight away, in warmed bowls.

Mixed Ravioli with Spring Vegetables

SERVES 6 as a starter; 4 as a main course

Ravioli is one of those foods that is often on offer in the supermarket, and it also freezes beautifully. The array of different fillings available is quite exciting, and when I have enough people at my table to eat their way through several packets, I buy an assortment of fillings. It makes every bite seem a bit of an adventure, a *delicious* adventure. Choose between cheese, meat, spinach, wild mushroom, asparagus, etc.

Adding a selection of spring-time vegetables to almost any pasta sauce makes a very impressive dish, and the truth is that you don't need many of each vegetable to make a splash. A small handful of little green asparagus tips, a few morsels of courgette and/or yellow summer squash, a few leaves of spinach and a scattering of peas and broad beans does the trick!

1 onion, chopped
4 cloves garlic, chopped
3 tablespoons olive oil
2 × 400g/14oz cans chopped tomatoes
salt and pepper
pinch of sugar (if needed)
½ teaspoon mixed Italian herbs or
   herbes de Provence
2–3 tablespoons tomato paste
10 young asparagus tips
60–90g/2–3oz young peas and peeled
   broad beans, blanched
8–10 spinach leaves, coarsely cut into
   pieces

2–3 × 350g/12oz packets (each serving
   2–3 people) vegetable, cheese or
   meat ravioli, or other stuffed pasta
1–2 tender young courgettes or other
   small tender squash, diced

To serve
30–60g/1–2oz Parmesan or similar
   cheese, freshly grated
fresh basil or marjoram leaves, finely
   shredded
olive oil

◆ Lightly sauté the onion and garlic in the olive oil in a saucepan for 5–10 minutes or until softened, then stir in the tomatoes (with their juices), salt, pepper, sugar (if needed to balance the acidity), herbs and tomato paste. Simmer for 5–10 minutes, then taste and adjust the seasoning, if necessary. Add the asparagus, peas, broad beans and spinach, and continue to simmer while you cook the pasta.

◆ Cook the pasta with the courgettes in rapidly boiling salted water until the pasta is *al dente* (see page 72). Drain, return to the saucepan and add the tomato-sauced vegetables. Toss well, then turn out on to a platter and scatter with fresh basil or marjoram, Parmesan or similar cheese and a drizzle of olive oil.

Vietnam-inspired Tomato–Spring Onion Noodles

SERVES 6 as a starter; 4 as a main course

Simple to prepare, this dish of Chinese noodles in a tomato and spring onion sauce, inspired by Vietnamese flavours, makes a zesty side dish or bed for seafood or meat, and if spring onions are cheap, it is a pleasure to make.

2 bunches spring onions, thinly sliced
3 tablespoons vegetable oil
5 cloves garlic, chopped
1½–2 teaspoons chopped fresh ginger
1½ × 400g/14oz can chopped tomatoes
a pinch of sugar

soy sauce to taste
1½–2 x 350g/12oz packets dried
    Chinese egg noodles
2 tablespoons chopped fresh coriander
    to garnish

◆ Heat the spring onions in the vegetable oil in a saucepan over a medium heat. Do not let them brown, but just warm them through until they wilt.

◆ Spoon the onions on to a plate, leaving the oil in the saucepan. Add the garlic and ginger, and cook for a few moments over a medium heat, then add the tomatoes, cooking over a medium heat until most of the liquid has evaporated. Add a pinch of sugar to balance the acidity of the tomatoes, and season with soy sauce. Add the wilted onions and set aside.

◆ Cook the noodles according to packet directions or until they are just tender, then drain and return to the pan. Toss lightly with a few shakes of soy sauce, then toss with the tomato sauce and serve straight away, sprinkled with coriander.

Chinese Noodle Bowl with Bean Sprouts, Carrots and Peanuts

SERVES 6 as a starter; 4 as a main course

Hoisin sauce adds a sweet-spicy Chinese flavour to anything it touches, so your initial expenditure adds flavour to your table for many meals.

Vegetables in season can be added to this noodle bowl: bok choy and broccoli are especially good.

Other nuts are delicious with this stir-fry, such as almonds and cashews, but peanuts are delightfully cheap. Finally, if you like a bit of spice, shake a little Tabasco into the sauce.

350g/12oz pork mince or 300g/10oz firm tofu, diced

4 cloves garlic, chopped

1–2 teaspoons chopped fresh ginger

2 tablespoons vegetable oil

1 bunch spring onions, thinly sliced

1 tablespoon sugar

1 teaspoon light soy sauce, or to taste, plus extra for tossing with the cooked noodles

5–6 tablespoons hoisin sauce (or more, to taste)

a sprinkling of Chinese five-spice powder

60–75ml/2–2½fl oz water

125g/4oz bean sprouts

500g/1lb dried Chinese egg noodles

2 teaspoons toasted (oriental) sesame oil, or to taste

3–4 tablespoons roasted (preferably dry-roasted) peanuts

1 carrot, cut into fine julienne

1 cucumber, cut into fine julienne

2–3 tablespoons coarsely chopped fresh coriander

- Stir-fry the pork mince or tofu with the garlic and ginger in the oil in a large frying pan or wok for 6–7 minutes or until lightly browned in places. Stir in half the spring onions, the sugar, soy sauce, hoisin sauce and five-spice powder. Remove the pan from the heat and stir in the water, then warm through for a few moments over a medium heat. Remove from the heat and add the bean sprouts.

- Cook the noodles in rapidly boiling salted water according to the directions on the packet or until they are just tender. Drain and toss with sesame oil, then serve straight away, each portion of noodles topped with some of the hot sauce, a sprinkling of the remaining spring onions, the peanuts, carrot and cucumber, and the coriander leaves.

Spaghetti Arrabbiata with Mussels

SERVES 6 as a starter; 4 as a main course

Chilli-spiked tomato sauce is known as 'arrabbiata'. Almost anything goes as far as this sauce is concerned, as long as it has a spicy kick.

If you are feeling rich beyond your means, add a handful of assorted seafood to the dish: thinly sliced squid, a few prawns, a scallop or two. With no seafood at all, however, the sauce is a triumph of frugality. If the wolf is at your door, omit the mussels and serve the spaghetti with only its spicy sauce.

When sautéeing the chilli, note that it will transmit more heat if broken up or crushed; whole it will add flavour but not too much fire. The choice is yours.

10–12 cloves garlic, 2 chopped, the rest sliced

1–2 dried red chillies, crushed or left whole (see above)

24 mussels in their shells, scrubbed and beards removed

6 tablespoons olive oil

2 × 400g/14oz can chopped tomatoes

60g/2oz or about 4–5 heaped table-spoons tomato paste

salt and black pepper

pinch of sugar (if needed)

a few generous pinches of dried oregano or other dried Mediterranean herb

500–625g/1¼lb spaghetti

2–3 tablespoons chopped fresh parsley

- Set aside the chopped garlic, and heat the sliced garlic, chillies and mussels in the olive oil for 3–4 minutes, taking care not to inhale the pungent fumes of the chillies or to let the garlic brown or burn (which will give the dish a bitter taste).

- Add the tomatoes and tomato paste, then cook over a high heat until they reduce to a thick saucy consistency, and the mussels have opened. Discard any mussels that are still shut. Season with salt, pepper, a pinch of sugar (if needed to balance the acidity), the reserved chopped garlic and the oregano. Set aside and keep warm while you cook the pasta.

- Cook the spaghetti rapidly in boiling salted water until just *al dente* (see page 72). Drain and return to the saucepan. Spoon the spicy tomato sauce over the cooked spaghetti, keeping back the mussels. Toss the sauce and spaghetti together, then tip into a warmed serving bowl and heap the mussels on top. Sprinkle with parsley and serve straight away.

Pasta with Pan-griddled Tomatoes and Rosemary–Parsley Oil

SERVES 6 as a starter; 4 as a main course

Pan-grilling, griddling or quickly charring the tomatoes in a hot frying pan, gives them an added layer of flavour, and cooks them through … barely. They still have a nice freshness and simplicity, though their texture is veering towards sauce-like. After cooking the tomatoes, the pan is deglazed with dry white wine, which is poured over the tomatoes before they are combined with the hot pasta and rosemary–parsley oil.

If you have a glass of leftover wine languishing in your kitchen, as I had when I came up with this recipe, this dish is the soul of economy. If I have a little basil growing on my windowsill I add that, too; if not, there's no need to purchase it specially – leave it out.

I like the fact that this recipe doesn't need cheese – just the pure, strong flavours of tomatoes and herbs, combined with satisfying mouthfuls of chewy pasta.

25–30 sweet, flavourful cherry
   tomatoes, halved
90ml/3fl oz extra virgin olive oil
sea salt
a pinch or two of sugar
350ml/12fl oz dry white wine
3 tablespoons very fresh young fragrant
   rosemary

2 tablespoons chopped fresh parsley
5–8 cloves garlic, coarsely chopped
several generous pinches of crushed red
   chillies or cayenne pepper
500–625 g/1-1¼lb pasta of choice
3 tablespoons fresh basil leaves,
   coarsely chopped (optional)

♦ Heat a griddle pan or heavy frying pan to medium hot. Place the tomatoes in the pan, cut sides down first, and drizzle them with a little olive oil. Cook, turning once or twice and sprinkling with salt and sugar, until the tomatoes begin to char in places. Continue cooking until they are marked with black and the skin is lightly charred but the tomatoes are still holding their shape, although a little soft. Remove from the pan and pour in the wine.

♦ Cook the wine over a medium-high heat until it boils down to no more than several tablespoons of liquid. Stir to scrape up the bits of tomato flesh and solidified juices so that they will cook into the wine. Pour the liquid over the tomatoes and set aside.

◆ In a mortar and pestle if possible, crush the rosemary until it is in quite small pieces, then add the parsley, garlic, crushed chillies or cayenne pepper, and a pinch or two of sea salt. Grind together, then work in the remaining olive oil to produce a chunky pesto-like sauce, though the herbs will be separated from the oil somewhat.

◆ Cook the pasta in rapidly boiling salted water until *al dente* (see page 72), then drain and return to the hot pan. Add the tomatoes and their juices with the herbal oil mixture, and toss together with the pasta. Heat for a few moments until heated through, then serve straight away, sprinkled with a little fresh basil, if desired.

A FEW RESTAURANT TRICKS

• Use pesto as a flavourful garnish on the plate. When the sauced food is mixed with it, layers of flavour are created. The green paste is also very appealing to look at.

• Use crisp-tender green beans as a garnish: stick them whole into a mound of mashed potatoes or hummus as a sort of flying saucer/spaceage presentation; scatter them around a barbecued steak; toss them with a plate of salad leaves. Ditto for chives.

• Edible flowers, especially herb blossoms, were a fashion cliché not long ago, but they are still beautiful and delicious and, as such, a delightful classic. Be sure that the flowers you choose are unsprayed and edible. Chive blossoms are pale purple pompoms and taste vaguely oniony; rosemary blossoms are lavender coloured, too, but delicate and small; rose petals are familiar to all of us; pansies are brightly coloured and more velvety in texture than any other flavour quality they have, nasturtiums are gaily coloured and taste bracingly of watercress.

• Carve cucumber lengths into little cups and fill them with a spicy relish or condiment.

Chickpea Ravioli with Ginger and Tomato Sauce

SERVES 6 as a starter; 4 as a main course

This truly cross-cultural ravioli, filled with puréed chickpeas and served with a ginger and tomato sauce, is full of bright flavour. Using wonton wrappers to make ravioli turns even the most humble mashed chickpea into an exciting dish (mashed potatoes, highly seasoned or spiced, also make a good filling). Purchase the wrappers in a Chinese grocery and keep a packet in your freezer to defrost as you like. Making and rolling the pasta yourself, of course, costs even less, but takes a lot more time and effort.

350g/12oz cooked chickpeas (1½ × 400g/14oz can chickpeas, drained and well rinsed)
6 cloves garlic, chopped
6 tablespoons ricotta or plain fromage frais
pinch each of dried mixed herbs and cumin seeds
1½ tablespoons chopped fresh parsley
about 4 heaped tablespoons freshly grated Parmesan

42–48 wonton wrappers
60ml/2fl oz extra virgin oil
10–12 fresh ripe tomatoes, chopped, or 1½ × 400g/14oz cans chopped tomatoes, strained and juice reserved
salt and pepper
pinch of sugar
2–3 teaspoons chopped fresh ginger
2–3 tablespoons fresh coriander leaves

♦ Purée the chickpeas in a food processor until they are a coarse, slightly chunky meal, then add half the garlic, the ricotta or fromage frais, the herbs, cumin and parsley, and purée again. Add enough Parmesan to make a thick paste consistency.

♦ Place one wonton wrapper flat on a work surface and wet the edges. Place 1–2 teaspoons of the chickpea mixture in the centre, then cover with a second wrapper and pinch the edges together, pressing them tightly and evenly to seal them well. Place the finished ravioli on a lightly floured plate and leave to stand while you finish making the sauce.

- To make the sauce, heat the remaining garlic in the olive oil for only a moment or until it is fragrant, then add the chopped tomatoes. If using canned tomatoes, add the tomatoes first, then when they have cooked down and separated from the oil, add the juice. Cook for about 5 minutes over a high heat until the sauce is reduced and flavourful. Season with salt, pepper and sugar (to balance the acidity of the tomatoes), and add the ginger. Taste for seasoning and remove from the heat.

- Cook the ravioli gently in a large, wide saucepan of simmering water so that they cook through but do not boil furiously and fall apart. This will only take about 3 minutes and, depending on the size of your pan, may need to be done in batches. (If you crowd the pan the ravioli will stick together.)

- Spoon a little of the hot sauce on to serving plates, top with the ravioli, then some more of the sauce. Serve sprinkled with coriander.

EXTRA PARMESAN FLAVOUR

A piece of Parmesan cheese rind adds extra cheese flavour, and would otherwise be thrown away. Save the rinds left after grating Parmesan or other grana-type cheese and keep them loosely wrapped in the refrigerator. When you make risotto, lentil soup or minestrone, simply add a piece of rind to the simmering mixture, then fish it out before serving (although many people like to chew on it, myself included, so ask before you toss it away).

Main Courses

6

Main Courses

...the central part of
the meal, enjoyed
when all are ready for
some serious eating...

Main Courses

PART of the fun of entertaining is structuring the meal in any way you think will be the most wonderful, taking into consideration life's practicalities. Sometimes, serving a selection of little dishes seems just right for the main course, as you might find for a Cypriot meze, or even a tapas crawl. Often, though, entertaining meals are at their best when the main course is the central part of the meal, enjoyed as everyone is settling in after the more light-hearted first course is finished, and all are ready for some serious eating.

In addition to the dishes that appear in this chapter, have a trawl through the rest of the book for soups, pasta, egg and cheese dishes that also make satisfying main courses.

Cumin-grilled Mackerel

SERVES 6

This is excellent North African fare for a sultry summer supper, especially accompanied by pan-grilled or barbecued aubergine slices and peppers, crisp olive-oil-fried potatoes, and a chilli sauce, such as harissa (pages 93 and 108) or Tabasco, to sprinkle on for an extra 'kick'.

Mackerel is an endearingly cheap fish, though its distinctive flavour really needs strong spicing to be delicious. I like this traditional paste of cumin, garlic, coriander and chilli, which is rubbed into the flesh of the fish.

1.5kg/3lb whole mackerel, gutted, cleaned and heads removed	4 heaped tablespoons chopped fresh coriander
90ml/3fl oz extra virgin olive oil	½–1 fresh red chilli, chopped, or ½–1
1 heaped tablespoon ground cumin	teaspoon harissa or Tabasco sauce
8 cloves garlic, crushed with ½–1 teaspoon salt	2 lemons or limes, cut into wedges, to serve

◆ Cut 2–3 deep diagonal slashes on each side of each fish and set them aside.

◆ Mix together the olive oil, cumin, crushed garlic, coriander and chilli or chilli sauce. Spoon some of the marinade into each slash, then rub the rest all over the fish. Leave to marinate for 30–60 minutes, or 2–3 hours in the refrigerator.

◆ Start a fire in the barbecue or heat the grill to high. Cook the fish over the hot coals or under the hot grill for about 8 minutes on each side, depending on the thickness of the fish. Serve hot, each portion accompanied by wedges of lemon or lime.

TWO FOR THE PRICE OF ONE

Often, ingredients – pesto, pasta, rice, mustards, spices, etc. – are sold in two-for-the-price-of-one special offers. Buy two whether you need them or not, and sell the other at half price, or swap it with a friend for something you *do* need, or give it to your neighbour as a gift.

Whole Fish with Preserved Lemon and Green Olives

SERVES 6

This dish is simple to prepare and a traditional speciality of Moroccan Jews. It's a good excuse to make a big batch of preserved lemons (see page 130), or to use up the ones you already have on your shelf, but if you don't have any or are not in the mood, use a combination of fresh lemons and a little bottled lemon juice. Though the latter can be quite harsh when used on its own, it adds that slight preserved-lemon flavour that is so appealing in many Moroccan dishes. Choose either Middle-Eastern or pimiento-stuffed Spanish olives. If using fish stock (which is salty) instead of water, you may wish to blanch your olives briefly in boiling water before using, to remove some of the saltiness.

1 whole fish, such as red snapper, or 1kg/2lb fillets
1 tablespoon ground cumin
2 teaspoons paprika
½ teaspoon ground ginger
½–1 teaspoon ground turmeric
½ teaspoon chilli seasoning, such as cayenne pepper, crushed dried red chillies or a hot sauce such as Tabasco
6 cloves garlic, chopped

2 tablespoons lemon juice or juice of 1 lemon
1–2 preserved lemons, diced, plus 1–2 tablespoons of the preserving liquid (see page 130)
4 tomatoes, chopped
½ bunch fresh coriander, chopped
125ml/4fl oz water or fish stock (made using ½ fish stock cube)
25–30 green olives (see above)

- Place the fish in a baking tin and coat on both sides with cumin, paprika, ginger, turmeric, chilli seasoning or sauce, garlic and lemon juice. Leave to stand for 30 minutes.

- Preheat the oven to 180°C/350°F/Gas Mark 4. Stir the preserved lemons with their liquid, the tomatoes, half the coriander and the water or fish stock into the tin, and bake for about 20 minutes or until the fish is beginning to cook through. Add the olives and continue cooking for another 10 minutes. Serve sprinkled with the remaining coriander.

Vietnamese Five-spice Marinated Barbecued Salmon

SERVES 6

Five-spice marinade is a traditional Vietnamese way of marinating and barbecuing poultry; in the streets of Saigon you find stalls selling all sorts of birds, marinated and cooked over hot coals. The spices permeate and tenderize, while keeping the meat juicy. Here I've used the marinade to oomph up the flavour of farmed salmon.

6 salmon steaks (farmed is most affordable), 500–750g/1–1½lb in total weight

5 cloves garlic, chopped

2 tablespoons each of demerara or light brown soft sugar, soy sauce or fish sauce, and dry sherry

1 tablespoon Chinese five-spice powder

3 spring onions, thinly sliced

several generous pinches of freshly ground black pepper

1 tablespoon sesame oil

1–2 tablespoons vegetable oil

• Combine the salmon with the garlic, brown sugar, soy sauce or fish sauce, dry sherry, five-spice powder, spring onions, black pepper and sesame oil. Leave to marinate for between 30 minutes and 2 hours at room temperature, or overnight in the refrigerator.

• Start a fire in the barbecue or heat the grill. Blot the salmon with absorbent kitchen paper to remove any excess marinade, then brush or drizzle well with vegetable oil.

• Grill or cook over hot coals for 2–3 minutes on each side, taking care not to overcook. Ideally the steaks should be nearly seared on the outside and quite rare inside. Serve hot.

Opposite page 88: Whole Fish with Preserved Lemon and Green Olives (page 88)
Opposite: Pork with Pink Peppercorns and Garlic Cream (page 105)

Bacon-wrapped Roasted Cod with Sage and Braised Cabbage

SERVES 6

Enclosing the fish in bacon is a great way of adding extra flavour while keeping the fish moist with a gentle basting of bacon fat. It looks nice too, all wrapped up like a present.

6 fillets or steaks of cod, or other firm-fleshed white fish, each weighing about 175g/6oz (1kg/2¼lb total weight)
6 cloves garlic, chopped
4 tablespoons olive oil
salt and black pepper
about 16 fresh sage leaves
12 rindless unsmoked streaky bacon rashers

3 tablespoons plain flour
1 medium onion, chopped
2 carrots, diced
½ head curly-leaf (Savoy) cabbage, shredded
250ml/8fl oz dry white wine
juice and grated zest of 1 lemon
250ml/8fl oz chicken or fish stock
2 tablespoons chopped fresh parsley

◆ Sprinkle the cod with half the garlic, 1 tablespoon of the olive oil and black pepper to taste. Top each steak with two sage leaves, then wrap in two bacon rashers, securing them if needed with a cocktail stick or two. Dust each parcel with flour. Preheat the oven to 220°C/425°F/Gas Mark 7.

◆ Heat 1 tablespoon of the remaining olive oil in a heavy frying pan, and sauté the remaining garlic with the onion and carrots for 5–10 minutes or until the vegetables are just softened. Add the cabbage and stir well to coat it all in the garlicky oil. Cook, stirring, for about 8 minutes or until the cabbage is softened. Remove the vegetables to a plate or bowl, along with their juices.

◆ Rinse the frying pan quickly with a little water, then heat 2 tablespoons of the remaining olive oil and sear the fish parcels, working in several batches to avoid crowding the pan. Cook over a medium-high heat for about 2 minutes on each side or until browned. As the parcels are cooked, transfer them to a large baking sheet, taking care they do not touch.

♦ Add the wine, lemon juice and lemon zest to the same frying pan (this time without rinsing) and cook over a high heat until reduced, then add the stock and continue to cook over a high heat until the liquid has reduced again to about half. Return the vegetables to the pan, add the parsley, lower the heat, cover, and cook over a medium heat for about 10 minutes or until the vegetables are quite soft. Meanwhile, roast the bacon-wrapped cod in the oven for about 10 minutes or until just cooked through. Chop the remaining sage leaves and stir them in to the cabbage with salt and pepper to taste.

♦ Arrange the cabbage in mounds on heated serving plates. Remove the cocktail sticks, if using, from the bacon-wrapped cod, and set each fish portion on a mound of cabbage. Serve straight away.

BACON BITS

Bits of bacon, the ends that haven't sold and are piled into a tray at a butcher's to sell at a special reduced price, are brilliant for the entertaining cook who is counting pennies. They are utterly delicious, and their irregular shapes and sizes, and rustic and varied texture, make them far more interesting than the assembly-line sameness of rashers. In addition to using them in salads, they are wonderful for simmering with lentils, beans or cabbage, including in stuffings, or adding to a pot of choucroute (sauerkraut). They can also be used to top refried beans and are perfect in pasta dishes such as Tagliatelle with Chicken Livers (page 74) and Pasta Shells with Tomato, Bacon and Oregano (page 73).

Sticky Mustard-spicy Chicken Wings with Portuguese Flavours

SERVES 6

Chicken wings are still pretty cheap, bless 'em, and few parts of the chicken are as tempting! All that crisp skin is irresistible, and it is impossible to eat them with a knife and fork: you are forced to use your fingers and will inevitably end up giving them a lick and smacking your lips. Great for breaking the ice, as it's hard to be reserved when you are busy smearing your lips with chicken drippings!

1.5kg/3lb chicken wings
3 tablespoons lemon or lime juice
1 teaspoon each of ground cumin and
  cinnamon
1 teaspoon dried basil or marjoram

3 tablespoons paprika
salt and pepper
4–5 tablespoons mild Dijon or whole
  grain mustard
3 tablespoons olive oil

- Cut the chicken wings into two pieces each, separating them at the joints. This will give you a tiny drumstick and a bonier, pointed part, and promotes even cooking, but separating them is not essential.

- Combine the chicken wings with the remaining ingredients and leave them as long as you can. Overnight in the refrigerator is best of all, but 1 hour isn't bad, and even 30 minutes gives good flavour to the little wings.

- Preheat the oven to 190°C/375°F/Gas Mark 5. Place the wings on a baking sheet and bake in the oven for 35–40 minutes, turning every so often for even baking, until the wings are crisp and browned. Raise the heat to 200–220°C/400–425°F/Gas Mark 6–7 and cook for a further 10 minutes, if necessary.

- Serve hot, though the wings are equally tasty when they have cooled to room temperature.

Spicy Chicken Brochettes with Green Olive Harissa

SERVES 6

Harissa is the ubiquitous hot red chilli sauce of North Africa, spiked with cumin, sometimes caraway seed and ginger, blistering with the heat of the chilli. This harissa is unique in its addition of chopped green olives – try it with roasted fish or barbecued fish kebabs as well as with chicken. Serve this luscious dish with accompanying couscous, or with steamed rice or crusty baguette.

1.25kg/2½lb boneless chicken thighs, skinned and cut into bite-sized chunks
2 tablespoons each of paprika and mild red chilli powder
1 teaspoon each of ground cumin and cayenne pepper
¼ teaspoon ground ginger
½ teaspoon curry powder

8 cloves garlic, chopped
juice of 1 lemon
3 tablespoons extra virgin olive oil
125 ml/4 fl oz vegetable stock or water
10 pimiento-stuffed green olives, chopped
2 tablespoons chopped fresh coriander

◆ Combine the chicken with half the paprika, half the chilli powder, half the cumin, half the cayenne pepper, half the ginger, all of the curry powder, half the garlic, half the lemon juice and 2 tablespoons of the olive oil. Leave to marinate for between 30 minutes and 2 hours at cool room temperature, or overnight in the refrigerator.

◆ Mix the remaining paprika, chilli powder, cumin, cayenne pepper and ginger in a saucepan with the stock or water. Bring to the boil, then remove from the heat and stir in the remaining garlic, lemon juice, olives and olive oil. Leave to cool.

◆ Light a fire in the barbecue, heat the grill to high, or heat a griddle pan. Thread the chicken on to metal or soaked bamboo skewers and cook on the barbecue, under the grill or in the griddle pan until the brochettes are just firm to the touch, lightly browned in places and slightly opaque. Do not overcook. Remove to a platter, sprinkle with coriander, and serve with the green olive harissa.

Tomato, Ginger and Cardamom Chicken

SERVES 6

This dish of chicken stewed in an Ethiopian-inspired tomato sauce is spicy and aromatic. Serve in shallow soup bowls with warm flour tortillas, pitta or naan breads to dip into the spicy sauce. For a more budget-minded, and I think more interesting, accompaniment, serve it with plain cooked risotto-like barley; its blandness is very nice with the spicy sauce.

Begin the meal with a starter of roasted peppers, or hot roasted feta cheese with peppers and tomatoes and a salad of shredded lettuce, cucumber, onions, garlic, carrots, lemon juice and hot chilli, with salt to taste – no oil at all!

juice of 1 lime or lemon
12 chicken thighs, with or without
   bones, skinned
salt and black pepper
2 tablespoons vegetable oil
3 large or 5 small to medium onions,
   chopped
2–3 teaspoons cardamom pods
2–3 teaspoons chopped fresh ginger

1–2 teaspoons mild chilli powder (or
   ancho or pasilla chilli powder)
5–6 cloves garlic, chopped
1 litre/32fl oz chicken stock
400g/14oz can chopped tomatoes
½ teaspoon ground turmeric
4 tablespoons chopped fresh coriander
4 pitas or naan breads or 8 flour
   tortillas, to serve

- Squeeze half the lime or lemon over the chicken, sprinkle with salt and pepper and leave to stand while you brown the onions.

- Heat the oil in a frying pan and slowly and lightly fry the onions over a low to medium heat until they are soft and golden brown in spots. Stir in the cardamoms, ginger and chilli, and cook for a few moments longer.

- Dry the chicken thighs with absorbent kitchen paper, and add them to the pan with the garlic. Cook with the spices over a medium-low heat for about 10 minutes, turning every so often and letting the chicken colour from the heat and chilli. Add the stock, tomatoes (with their juices) and turmeric, and simmer until the chicken thighs are tender, taking care not to overcook them. Boneless thighs will take a short time to cook, perhaps 10–15 minutes, while thighs on the bone will be enhanced by a longish slow simmer, say 30 minutes. Remove

the chicken from the pan and place in shallow soup bowls. Taste the
sauce for seasoning, and add the rest of the lemon or lime juice.

◆ Pour a ladleful into each bowl, sprinkle with the fresh coriander, and
serve accompanied by triangles of pitta or naan, or flour tortillas.

'Jerked' Chicken Thighs

SERVES 6

Jerk is a Caribbean mixture of spices, thyme and fiery Scotch bonnet chillies,
rubbed on to meat, fish or poultry, then left to marinate before being barbecued.
It is available in paste or dried forms. The spicy marinade gives such a great flavour
to the meat that it tastes just as good cooked in a griddle pan on the hob.
Economical chicken thighs are perfect for 'jerking', but pork and lamb are also
good, either in individual cutlets or chops, or large roast-like cuts for slow cooking. Fattier, cheaper cuts work best for this as they can cook for longer, with their
fat basting the meat, while it all grows tender over the smoky fire.

12 boneless chicken thighs, with or
   without skin
4 tablespoons lime or lemon juice
3 tablespoons demerara sugar
5 cloves garlic, chopped
2 tablespoons soy sauce
3 tablespoons brandy, sherry or rum
1 bunch spring onions, thinly sliced
1–2 tablespoons jerk seasoning spice

1 teaspoon ground allspice
1 teaspoon chopped fresh ginger
½–1 teaspoon ground cinnamon
½ teaspoon freshly grated nutmeg
1 tablespoon chopped fresh thyme
60ml/2fl oz olive oil or vegetable oil
salt and coarsely ground black pepper
½–1 fresh green chilli, chopped

◆ Mix the chicken and all the other ingredients together and leave to
marinate in the refrigerator, well covered, for 1–2 days and nights.

◆ Bring the chicken mixture to room temperature before cooking. Light
a fire in the barbecue, heat the grill to high, heat a griddle pan on the
hob, or heat a little oil in a heavy frying pan, and cook the chicken
until it is brown and crusty on the outside and cooked through.

Spicy Roasted Mexican Chicken Legs

SERVES 6

Drumsticks are great for informal entertaining, especially stand-up buffets, as they conveniently come with their own bone-handle to hold them by. Here the legs are marinated in chilli spices, then wrapped in bacon rashers and baked, though you can cook them over a barbecue instead. Removing the skin lets the spicy marinade permeate the meat, and the streaky bacon wrapping bastes the chicken as it cooks.

6–8 cloves garlic, chopped
1 tablespoon each of ground cumin,
   paprika and mild or hot chilli powder
juice of ½ orange
grated zest of ¼ orange
juice of ½ lemon or lime

2 tablespoons olive oil
salt and pepper
½ fresh chilli, chopped
12 chicken drumsticks, skinned
12 smoked streaky bacon rashers

◆ Combine the garlic, cumin, paprika, chilli powder, orange juice and zest, lemon or lime juice, olive oil, salt and pepper to taste, and chilli, and smear it on to the chicken meat. Wrap each leg (the meat portion only) in a rasher of streaky bacon. Leave to marinate for at least 1 hour at room temperature, or up to 2 days in the refrigerator.

◆ When ready to cook, preheat the oven to 180°C/350°F/Gas Mark 4. Arrange the drumsticks in a baking dish, not letting the chicken pieces touch each other, and bake in the oven for 40–45 minutes or until the bacon is crispy and brown, and the chicken tender. Serve hot, or at room temperature for a picnic.

Mediterranean-flavoured Spatchcocked Chicken

SERVES 6

Chicken is so delicious, so versatile, so popular, and, at the risk of sounding boring, so darned cheap. Marinating brings out the best in any chicken. Take any 1kg/2lb bird and marinate it for 2 days, and you have a memorable dinner. Here

I have used a pounded mixture of garlic, fennel, oregano, parsley, olive oil and lemon, rubbed into a spatchcocked chicken. Leaving it for 2 days in the refrigerator, well-wrapped, allows the marinade to thoroughly permeate the flesh and keep it moist. 'Spatchcocking' the bird (that is, cutting through its backbone and flattening it, or simply cutting it into two halves) helps it to cook evenly and quickly, regardless of whether you grill, roast, barbecue or pan-fry it.

2 small chickens (about 1kg/2lb each)
10 cloves garlic
1 teaspoon salt
1 teaspoon fennel seeds
1 teaspoon dried oregano
6 tablespoons coarsely chopped fresh
   parsley

black pepper
grated zest of 1 lemon
juice of 2 lemons
5 tablespoons extra virgin olive oil
few sprigs of parsley or other fresh
   herbs to garnish

♦ Spatchcock the chickens for easy cooking: cut down one side of the backbones, then lay them flat and press on their breastbones to flatten them out. Using a sharp knife or kitchen shears, cut away the backbones.

♦ Crush the garlic in a mortar and pestle, blender or food processor with the salt, then add the fennel seeds, oregano, parsley, black pepper to taste, lemon zest, lemon juice and olive oil. Rub this mixture into the chickens, wrap them up in double plastic bags, and leave in the refrigerator for up to 2 days.

♦ When ready to cook, preheat the oven to 190°C/375°F/Gas Mark 5. Roast the chickens for about 20 minutes, then check to see if they are done by piercing the thighs with a skewer or sharp knife. If the juices that run out are clear, not pink, the chickens are cooked.

♦ To finish and crisp up the skin, place the chickens under the grill for 5–10 minutes or until the skin is crisp and the juices of the thigh run clear even if deeply pricked.

♦ Serve hot, carved into serving pieces, in the chickens' own flavourful juices, and garnished with a few sprigs of parsley or other fresh herbs.

Crusty Italian Countryside Breast of Lamb

SERVES 6-8

Breast of lamb is enticingly cheap, and one of the tastiest cuts of lamb for barbecuing or slow oven roasting. Marinating helps to tenderize and moisturize this flavourful meat. Serve with a gratin of aubergines, or with pasta and an invigorating salad.

2 breasts of lamb, trimmed and cut into chunks or slices between the pieces of bone

10 cloves garlic, chopped

3 teaspoons dried Mediterranean herbs, such as herbes de Provence or a mixture of Italian herbs, or 3 table-spoons chopped fresh rosemary

salt and black pepper

2 tablespoons olive oil

2 tablespoons vinegar, preferably balsamic, red wine or raspberry

250ml/8fl oz red wine

◆ Combine the lamb with all the other ingredients and leave at room temperature for 2–4 hours or overnight in the refrigerator.

◆ Remove the lamb from the marinade and blot dry with absorbent kitchen paper. If cooking on the barbecue, start a fire and, when the coals are white, place the lamb on the grill, not too close to the fire. Close the top of the barbecue, if possible, and let the meat cook over a low heat for an hour or longer, or until the meat is crusty, very tender, but not dry.

◆ If you are roasting your lamb instead of barbecuing, preheat the oven to 180°C/350°F/Gas Mark 4. Place the lamb in a large roasting tin, in a single layer if possible, and roast for about 2 hours or until it is tender.

◆ Remove the lamb from the fire or oven and serve straight away.

Note

For preparing ahead of time and easier serving, the meat can be half-cooked over the barbecue to impart the smoky flavour and aroma, then finished in the oven.

Marinated Barbecued Lamb with Citrus Mojo

SERVES 6

Mojo is a Cuban citrus-based sauce, redolent of garlic, and often quite thick with oil, too. I have cut back on the oil, and used both orange and lime juice as well as a hint of cumin for a lighter version. Other citrus juices can be used, too: grapefruit, ruby orange juice, tangerine juice, etc. Mojo is delicious with almost anything cooked on a grill or barbecue, especially a rich meat such as lamb, but you could try it on salmon, for the sunset colours and the refreshing citrus paired with the rich fish.

1kg/2lb lamb cutlets, such as from the
    shoulder, or 1.75kg/3½lb lamb breast
6 tablespoons olive oil
20 cloves garlic, thinly sliced
155ml/5fl oz orange juice

4 tablespoons lime juice
1 teaspoon ground cumin
1 teaspoon mild chilli powder
¼ teaspoon fresh oregano leaves
salt and black pepper

- Combine the lamb with half the olive oil, half the garlic, half the orange juice, half the lime juice and half the cumin. Add all the chilli powder and oregano, and salt and pepper to taste. Leave to marinate for 30–60 minutes, or overnight in the refrigerator.

- Heat the remaining olive oil in a saucepan and cook the remaining garlic until it turns golden but not brown. Add the remaining orange juice, lime juice and cumin, and cook it over a high heat for 2–3 minutes, or until the mixture is somewhat condensed but not evaporated away. If it threatens to do this, add a little water. Season with salt and black pepper, and set aside.

- If using lamb cutlets, grill, barbecue or pan-fry them for a few minutes on each side until browned on the outside and pink to ruddy inside. If using a large cut, like lamb breast or shoulder, roast in the oven at 180°C/350°F/Gas Mark 4 or over a medium heat in a barbecue (preferably covered), for 1–2 hours or until roasted and crusty on the outside and tender and well done within (see page 98 for barbecued lamb breast).

- Serve the lamb on plates with a puddle of the mojo sauce, or serve the mojo separately for each person to take as he or she desires.

Lamb and Charred Onions in Tortillas with Lime Pickle

SERVES 6

The onions and lamb for this can easily be made ahead of time, especially if you are having a barbecue the day before – the smoky scent will only enhance the spicy tortilla roll-ups. Whole cooked onions are often neglected in favour of chopped onions as an ingredient for sauces, stews or soups. Here they are charred, a technique I grew to love in Mexico; when sliced up they are delicate and sweet, a perfect foil for the shreds of hearty lamb.

350g/12oz boneless lamb cutlets, thinly sliced
3 cloves garlic, chopped
2 tablespoons chopped fresh rosemary
½ teaspoon cumin seeds
salt and pepper
2–3 tablespoons vegetable oil
1–2 teaspoons lemon juice, balsamic vinegar or red wine

3–4 medium to large onions, cut into halves crossways
12 flour tortillas
lime pickle
3–4 tablespoons fresh coriander leaves
4–6 tablespoons Greek yogurt (optional)

♦ Combine the lamb with the garlic, rosemary, cumin, salt and pepper to taste, 1 tablespoon oil and the lemon juice, balsamic vinegar or red wine. Set aside while you cook the onions.

♦ Heat a very lightly oiled, heavy frying pan and when it is quite hot, place the onions, cut sides down, on the hot surface. Cook until charred or lightly blackened, then turn them over and char the other sides. Lower the heat, cover, and cook the onions over a low heat for 5–8 minutes or until they are just tender, turning them every so often so that they cook evenly and do not burn in any one place. Remove the onions to a plate and slice lengthways. Season with salt and pepper and set aside, keeping them warm.

♦ Heat the remaining oil in a frying pan and stir-fry the lamb for about 5 minutes until it is browned but still pink inside. Work in several batches to avoid overcrowding the pan if you need to. Add the lamb to the onions.

◆ Warm the tortillas in either a heavy ungreased or lightly greased frying pan or a microwave until they are soft and warm. If warming them in a pan, sprinkle each one lightly with a few drops of water and warm them in a stack, turning them so that each is exposed to the heat. If using a microwave, warm them in a stack on a plate. When they are warm, wrap in a clean tea-towel.

◆ To make the roll-ups, take one tortilla and spread it with lime pickle, then with a few spoons of the meat and onion mixture, a sprinkling of coriander, and a few dabs of Greek yogurt if desired. Roll up, folding over the top and bottom first then roll from one side to keep the contents enclosed. Serve straight away.

MAKING THE MOST OF LEFTOVERS

Consider having two parties back to back one weekend: it's a good way of making use of the leftovers and of catching up on your entertaining. Make some extra Crusty Italian Countryside Breast of Lamb (page 98) and cut it into small pieces: include it next day in a salad. Or make extra Daube (page 102) and serve it with pasta and diced olives the next day. Leftover wine can enrich a wide variety of sauces; a nearly full bottle means you can have an almost painless Oeufs en Meurette (page 46) the next day.

Daube Provençal

SERVES 6 with leftovers (makes a big pot of
meaty stew)

When the weather is freezing and the nights are long and dark, I make a big
pot of a red winey stew and invite a tableful of guests to share it with me. Luckily,
this stew tastes best when cooked with the cheapest cuts, such as lamb shoulder,
shank or neck. A bottle of rustic red won't set you back too much, and you only
need the brandy if you have it to hand (don't go out of your way to buy a bottle,
though the scent of brandy does add a certain finesse to the dish). Serve the rich
stew with mashed potatoes if you feel like spending on butter and cream. If not,
steamed rice or crusty bread are quite good to sop up the savoury sauce, and a
good deal less heavy than those potatoes would be.

1.75–2.25kg/3½–4½lb lamb chunks,
  with bones still attached
2 tablespoons brandy (optional)
1 bottle red wine
1 bulb garlic, roughly cut up
1 onion, coarsely chopped
peel from ¼ orange or 1 tangerine,
  clementine or satsuma, cut into small
  pieces
½ teaspoon dried herbes de Provence
  (including a pinch of both fennel seeds
  and lavender)

several grindings of black pepper
2 tablespoons olive oil
60g/2oz bacon bits or 2 rindless
  smoked bacon rashers, chopped
2 teaspoons flour
3 carrots, diced
1 leek, diced
½ turnip, diced (optional)
400g/14oz can chopped tomatoes
2–3 tablespoons chopped fresh herbs,
  such as parsley, basil, rosemary, thyme
  or whatever is in season, to serve.

◆ Combine the meat with the brandy, if using, red wine, garlic, onion,
  citrus peel, herbes de Provence and black pepper. Leave to stand for
  4 hours at room temperature or overnight in the refrigerator.

◆ Remove the meat from its marinade, reserving the marinade, and dry
  the meat with absorbent kitchen paper. Heat the olive oil in a heavy
  frying pan or flameproof casserole and brown the meat with the bacon
  bits, cooking in batches until all the meat is lightly browned. Toss the
  meat with the flour.

◆ Pour off any fat that remains in the bottom of the pan, and return the meat to the casserole with the flour it is tossed with. Add the vegetables from the marinade, then strain the marinade liquid to remove the sludgy residue, and pour over the meat. Add the carrots, leek, turnip, if using, and tomatoes. Bring the mixture to the boil, then cover it with a tight-fitting lid and either simmer it on a very low heat on the hob or cook it in the oven at 160°C/325°F/Gas Mark 3 for 2–3 hours or until the meat is very tender.

◆ When the meat is tender, pour off the sauce. Skim it of its fat, then boil it down until it reduces to a flavourful sauce. Return the sauce to the meat and warm through. Taste for seasoning, then serve hot, sprinkled with chopped fresh herbs.

SPLIT GREEN PEAS

An unusual twist to add interest to any simple stew of chicken, meat, aubergine, etc., is to add several tablespoons of split green peas that you have soaked for about an hour. They keep their shape and character as long as they don't overcook, yet they blend into the sauce and add a subtle background flavour and texture. And they hardly cost anything; you can always have a few tablespoons soaked and ready to use in your freezer.

Beef or Pork Escalopes with Shallot Confit

SERVES 6

Shallot confit, despite its rather elegant name, is merely a delectable pile of golden sautéed then simmered shallots. I ate this repeatedly in Parisian bistros last winter, the soft, golden oniony mixture blanketing simple grilled or pan-browned escalopes of meat (pork, beef or veal). Though beef flank steak, scored for tenderness, is a most delicious cut of meat in this dish, pork is of course the most economical. I also find that a small amount of meat is all I want with the rich onions, especially if I'm having Sautéed New Potatoes (page 120) alongside as well, which I definitely recommend. As usual, for the wine, I use whatever leftover wine is waiting in my refrigerator.

45g/1½oz butter	a grating of nutmeg
4 medium onions, thinly sliced	125ml/4fl oz dry white wine
250g/8oz shallots, sliced (see Note, over)	625–750g/1¼–1½lb escalopes of steak
salt and pepper	or pork, beef or veal

- In a very deep, heavy frying pan or flameproof casserole, melt 30g/1oz of the butter, and add the onions and shallots. Cover and sweat (lightly sauté) over a low heat for 15–20 minutes. Sprinkle with salt, pepper and nutmeg as they cook, which will help them to go limp and caramelise slightly.

- When the onions and shallots are soft and golden, remove the cover and pour in the wine. Cook until the wine evaporates, then slowly sauté a few minutes longer. You want the onions to be almost silky but not browned. Transfer the onions and shallots to a saucepan or bowl, and keep them warm while you cook the meat.

- Heat the remaining butter in the pan and cook the meat quickly, browning lightly on each side. If cooking beef, I suggest serving it rare; if pork, then cook it until it is completely done, that is slightly pink, not grey.

- Slice the meat on the diagonal and serve it blanketed with the warm golden onions. Accompany with sautéed potatoes, on the plate alongside, if liked.

Note

Shallots are expensive in supermarkets and greengrocer's. Indian shops often sell a type of tiny, round, purple-fleshed shallot (there are numerous types of shallot) very cheaply and they are delicious. Another cost-cutting trick for a shallot-rich dish like this is to use a combination of half onions and half shallots. Onions are almost always cheap and blend well with shallots.

Pork with Pink Peppercorns and Garlic Cream

SERVES 6

If you don't have pink peppercorns, sprinkle the dish with fresh tarragon, or any other herb that takes your fancy. If you feel rich, use both peppercorns and herbs!

750g/1½lb pork escalopes, chops or steaks
salt and pepper
30g/1oz butter
2 shallots or 1 onion, chopped
2 cloves garlic, chopped

350ml/12fl oz dry white wine
350ml/12fl oz double or single cream
1–2 teaspoons pink peppercorns and 1 tablespoon chopped fresh tarragon, parsley or other herb of choice, to serve

♦ Sprinkle the pork with salt and pepper. If the pieces are thick, slice them more thinly so that they cook more quickly.

♦ Heat half the butter in a deep frying pan or flameproof casserole, and cook the pork escalopes without crowding the pan for a few minutes on each side, or until they are just gilded and have changed colour. Remove to a plate. Heat the remaining butter in the same pan and add the shallots or onion and the garlic. Lightly sauté for about 5 minutes or until the onion is soft, then pour in the wine and cook over a high heat until it is reduced by at least half. Remove from the heat, stir in the cream, and return to a medium heat to cook down, stirring as it cooks and reduces.

♦ Return the pork to the simmering sauce, along with any of the juices that have accumulated on the plate. Warm through but do not over-cook. Serve sprinkled with pink peppercorns and tarragon, parsley or whichever herb you fancy.

Middle-Eastern Meatballs

SERVES 6

There is nothing quite so tasty, satisfying and 'budget' as meatballs. My favourite seasonings veer towards the Mediterranean, with lots of garlic picked up along the way. Eat meatballs browned, as in this following recipe, or stretch them out, the way the locals do, by simmering them with tomatoes and courgettes (or marrow), aubergine, peppers, spinach, chickpeas or whatever vegetable is plentiful.

Serve this dish with a pilaff that has raisins and almonds forked into it, some cooling yogurt and a plate of salady things: cucumbers, onions, mint leaves and dill.

1kg/2lb lean lamb mince
90–125g/3–4oz (3–4 slices) stale bread, broken into pieces or whirled into crumbs
5–8 cloves garlic, chopped
2 onions, finely chopped
1½ teaspoons each of ground cumin, curry powder and paprika

½ bunch fresh coriander or parsley, finely chopped
2 teaspoons tomato paste
2 tablespoons plain yogurt or single cream
salt and black pepper
crushed dried red chillies to taste
olive oil for frying

◆ Mix the lamb mince with the bread, garlic, onions, cumin, curry powder, paprika, coriander or parsley, tomato paste and yogurt or cream, and salt, black pepper and crushed chillies to taste. Chill until firm, then roll into balls. Heat a little olive oil in a frying pan and fry the meatballs for 10 minutes or until crisply browned. (If your first batch of meatballs fall apart somewhat as they cook, roll the remainder in flour before frying.)

◆ Remove from the pan and drain on absorbent kitchen paper before serving.

Gammon with Prunes and Creamy Port Pan Sauce

SERVES 6

This rich dish is only a frugal feast if you have some port-like wine lying around in the kitchen, and if you can buy cream and gammon at reduced prices.

For the port, there is usually something around that would otherwise have been chucked out: a glass of Mavrodaphne left in the bottle that someone brought as a gift; the last of the port left over from Christmas; a slurp of Madeira...

The sauce is creamy and sophisticated, scented with cinnamon and vanilla. The dab of tomato paste gives a tangy edge to the sauce; the type sold in tubes not only costs little, but saves you buying a new can each time you need a small amount, as it keeps well, tightly capped, in the refrigerator.

30g/1oz butter
750g/1½lb gammon, cut into 6 steaks
2 medium onions, chopped
350ml/12fl oz port, Madeira,
    Mavrodaphne or similar fortified wine
½ teaspoon red wine vinegar
250ml/8fl oz water
18 prunes, preferably stoned

5cm/2in cinnamon stick or several
    shakes of ground cinnamon
pinch of coarsely ground black pepper
2.5cm/1in vanilla pod or a few drops of
    vanilla essence flavouring
2 tablespoons tomato paste
560ml/18fl oz single or double cream

- Heat the butter in a frying pan and lightly brown the gammon steaks until they are just turning opaque, then turn and brown the second side. Remove the gammon to a plate.

- Add the onions, port or other wine, vinegar, water, prunes, cinnamon, pepper and vanilla pod, if using, to the pan. Bring to the boil and cook down over a high heat until the liquid has reduced and slightly thickened, and the onions have softened. Turn the heat down to very low. Stir in the tomato paste and cream, then return the gammon to the pan, cover and simmer over a low heat for 5–8 minutes or until the gammon is cooked through. Stir in the vanilla essence, if using, and remove the cinnamon stick and vanilla pod, if using. Serve straight away, or prepare ahead of time and warm through just before serving.

Vegetable Couscous

SERVES 6

A big platter of couscous, ladled with tender spicy stewed vegetables and a bowl of fiery hot harissa makes a terrific focal point for an entertaining meal. Couscous is one of those dishes that can stretch to feed a multitude: as long as your pans are big enough you can add another handful of vegetables, a bit more of the grains, simmer another pan of beans ... and the sociability of the dish is practically a party in itself.

2–3 tablespoons vegetable oil or olive oil, or a mixture of the two

1 onion, chopped

4–5 cloves garlic, chopped

1 tablespoon each of cumin seeds (or 2 teaspoons ground cumin) and paprika

¼–½ teaspoon each of ground ginger and curry powder or garam masala, (see Note over)

⅛–¼ teaspoon each of ground cinnamon, cloves, coriander and turmeric

4 fresh tomatoes, chopped, or 250g/8oz can chopped tomatoes

1.5 litres/2½ pints vegetable stock

3 carrots, cut into sticks

½ head cabbage, cut into bite-sized chunks

3 courgettes or 1 marrow, cut into sticks (about 350g/12oz total weight)

155g/5oz green or runner beans, cut into bite-sized lengths

250g/8oz cooked chickpeas (canned are fine)

6 hard-boiled eggs, shelled (optional)

500g/1lb couscous

155g/5oz raisins or sultanas

45g/1½oz butter

1–2 tablespoons orange flower or rose water (optional)

For the harissa

1 teaspoon each of ground cumin, paprika and crushed red chillies or cayenne pepper (or harissa paste sold in tubes and cans)

1–2 cloves garlic, chopped

1 tablespoon chopped fresh coriander

◆ Heat the oil in a large saucepan and add the onion and garlic. Lightly sauté for 5–10 minutes or until the onion is softened, then stir in the cumin, paprika, ginger, curry powder (or garam masala), cinnamon, cloves, coriander and turmeric, and cook for a few minutes to bring out the flavours of the spices; do not let it brown or burn. Add the tomatoes (with their juices if using canned), vegetable stock, carrots and cabbage, and bring to the boil, then reduce the heat, cover, and simmer over a low to medium heat for about 30 minutes, or until the vegetables are cooked through. Add the courgettes or marrow and green or runner beans and continue to cook until these vegetables too are tender. Add the chickpeas and eggs, if using, and cook to warm through and permeate with the flavours of the vegetable stew.

◆ While the vegetables are cooking, place the couscous and raisins or sultanas in a large baking dish. Moisten with about 125ml/4fl oz cold water and work it into the grains with your fingers. Leave the grains to swell for 5–10 minutes, then loosen them with your fingers, add more water and leave them to swell again.

◆ Meanwhile, to make the harissa, ladle 350ml/12fl oz hot stock out of the vegetable pan into a saucepan, and add the harissa spices. Bring to the boil and cook for 5 minutes, taking care not to inhale the pungent steam. Stir in the garlic and coriander, and if you prefer a very hot harissa, add extra cayenne pepper, harissa paste or hot pepper seasoning (Encona or Tabasco).

◆ Transfer the couscous to a large saucepan. Bring the heat of the cooking vegetables up to nearly boiling, then ladle about 500ml/16fl oz of the stock on to the couscous. Mix well, then cover and cook over a very low heat for a few minutes. Check to see if the grains are moist and tender enough; if not add more hot stock.

◆ When the grains are tender, fluff them up with a fork, add the butter and toss well, then add a sprinkling of orange flower or rose water, if liked. Mound the couscous on a huge serving platter.

◆ Drain the vegetables, reserving the remaining stock, and serve them either piled appealingly on the couscous or in a separate bowl, accompanied by a jug of the hot stock for moistening the couscous with as you eat, and a bowl of the hot and spicy harissa for each person to add as they desire.

Note

Curry powder is not a Moroccan seasoning, but the mixture of spices in curry powder or garam masala, when combined with the other spices in the recipe, approximates to the Moroccan 'ras-el-hanout' spice mix.

Malaysian Curry of Autumn Vegetables with Tomatoes, Lemon and Basil

SERVES 6

I like to serve this with warm flour tortillas or soft warm naan breads to wrap up the vegetables and sauce. If you like tofu as much as I do, you'll probably want to include it as well. Simply stir-fry about 175g/6oz firm tofu, then add it to the stewing vegetables, taking care that it doesn't break up as the dish cooks.

3–5 dried shiitake mushrooms (see Note overleaf)

3 tablespoons dry-roasted peanuts

1 stalk lemon grass, finely chopped, or 1 teaspoon puréed lemon grass from a jar, or 2–3 teaspoons grated lemon zest

1 onion, chopped, or 4 shallots (see Note on page 105)

6 cloves garlic, chopped

2–3 fresh red chillies, chopped

6 tablespoons chopped fresh coriander (including the stems and roots if you like)

½ teaspoon ground turmeric

¼ teaspoon curry powder

2–3 tablespoons vegetable oil

½ aubergine, cut into bite-sized chunks

about 125g/4oz pumpkin or other autumn squash

2 potatoes, peeled and cut into bite-sized chunks

salt and pepper

350ml/12fl oz vegetable stock if using coconut milk; 500ml/16fl oz if using creamed coconut

250g/8oz runner beans or other green beans, cut into 2.5cm/1in lengths

400g/14oz can chopped tomatoes

250ml/8fl oz unsweetened coconut milk or 60–90g/2–3oz creamed coconut, slivered or cut into chunks

2 tablespoons lemon juice

several handfuls fresh basil, torn or coarsely chopped

♦ Rehydrate the dried shiitakes by placing them in a bowl with 250ml/ 8fl oz hot water. Leave to soak while you make the curry paste and cook the vegetables.

♦ To make the curry paste, put the peanuts, lemon grass or lemon zest, onion or shallots, garlic, red chillies, coriander, turmeric, curry powder and a tablespoon or two of the oil in a blender or food processor, or in a mortar and pestle, and grind together. Heat the remaining oil in a heavy frying pan, add the curry paste, and cook over a low heat for 7–8 minutes or until it is fragrant and the solids have separated from the oil.

- Add the aubergine, squash and potatoes, and cook for a few minutes in the paste and oil, then sprinkle in salt and pepper to taste and add the stock. Cook over a high heat for about 10 minutes, then add the runner or green beans and tomatoes, and continue to cook for a few more minutes, stirring to be sure the mixture cooks evenly.

- Remove the shiitakes from their soaking liquid. Strain the soaking liquid to rid it of grit and save the strained water for the sauce. Cut the rehydrated shiitakes into bite-sized pieces and add to the cooking vegetables with the strained soaking liquid. Continue to cook the vegetables for a few more minutes or until the beans are cooked through.

- Reduce the heat to a simmer and stir the coconut milk or creamed coconut into the sauce. Let it cook through with the vegetables for a few minutes and thicken the sauce, then stir in the lemon juice and basil. Serve straight away.

Note

Dried shiitakes can be costly when purchased in a supermarket or speciality shop. In Chinatown or a Chinese grocery, however, they are often very reasonable. Since they last nearly forever, stock up when you have a chance. You'll find yourself using them in all sorts of dishes, ranging from the Far Eastern to East–West and decidedly European, such as an Italian ragu or pasta. Their flavour is wonderful.

Light Vegetable Dishes and Accompaniments

7

Light Vegetable Dishes and Accompaniments

...rice, grains, beans and legumes; super-easy to prepare and strikingly delicious...

Light Vegetable Dishes and Accompaniments

NO longer straitjacketed in the way we serve and eat vegetables, we are delighting in our 'veg' as side dishes. I especially like the way the French serve them as a separate course in their own right, or the Italians call them 'contorni', that is, the food that forms the contours of the meal around the more basic meat or fish main courses. These contorni are often brought to the table at the beginning of the meal as appetizers, and remain there from the first course through the main course, for all to dip into at will and as desired.

Rice, grains, beans and legumes make wonderful accompaniments, and are the stars of the ethnic kitchen. They are also very chic – just take a look at modern restaurant menus in London, Paris, Milan or San Francisco.

Tomatoes à la Provençale

Make these when you have a glut of ripe, summery tomatoes and leftover stale bread. Not only are they good hot, but they are also good at room temperature, if not better. Any leftovers can be cut into bite-sized pieces and tossed with garlicky pasta as a quick impromptu sauce.

9–10 fresh, ripe, flavourful tomatoes
salt and a pinch of sugar
8 cloves garlic, chopped
about 250g/8oz breadcrumbs made
  from stale bread
black pepper
mixed herbs, such as herbes
  de Provence

1–2 tablespoons tomato paste or
  canned chopped tomatoes (optional)
several tablespoons freshly grated
  Parmesan cheese (optional)
6–8 tablespoons extra virgin olive oil
3–5 tablespoons chopped fresh herbs,
  such as basil, parsley, marjoram,
  rosemary, etc.

- Halve each tomato crossways and gently scoop out its seeds and some of its flesh, saving this fleshy pulp in a bowl. Sprinkle the insides of the tomatoes with salt and sugar, turn them upside down on a plate and leave to drain for 15–30 minutes. (You will add any juices that drain out to the breadcrumbs.) Preheat the oven to 220°C/425°F/Gas Mark 7.

- Arrange the tomatoes, cut sides up, on a baking sheet. Sprinkle about half the garlic over and inside them. Combine the remaining garlic with the breadcrumbs, tomato pulp, salt and pepper to taste, herbes de Provence to taste, tomato paste or canned chopped tomatoes, if using, Parmesan cheese, if using, and about half the olive oil and half the fresh herbs. Add the juices that have drained out of the tomatoes. Stuff this breadcrumb mixture into the hollowed-out tomato halves. Drizzle the tops with olive oil and bake in the oven for about 15 minutes or until the breadcrumbs are lightly browned in spots and the tomatoes seem somewhat tender. Remove from the oven, scatter the tops with the remaining chopped herbs and eat hot, or leave to cool and enjoy at room temperature.

Creamy Onion Gratin with the Scent of Bay Leaves

SERVES 6

For this warming winter dish, onions are simmered with bay leaves, then sliced up and layered with a modest amount of cream. This is a good dish to make in the winter when the richness is welcome, onions are cheap, and cream is often offered at a discount for holiday entertaining.

It is amazing how a dish as simple as an onion gratin can be so utterly delicious. Be sure to offer chunks of bread to sop up the savoury bits; I like to make the gratin in individual casseroles so that each person has his or her own crusty bits and can pick at them without self-consciousness.

10 medium onions, peeled but whole	freshly grated nutmeg
6–7 bay leaves	salt and pepper
8 shallots, chopped	8–10 tablespoons double cream

◆ Place the onions in a saucepan with the bay leaves and enough water to cover. Bring to the boil and simmer gently for about 20 minutes or until they are just tender but not mushy. Remove the onions and let cool. (Use the cooking liquid for something else: soup, sauces, braises, etc.) Preheat the oven to 190°C/375°F/Gas Mark 5.

◆ When the onions are cool enough to handle, slice them crossways into pieces about 1cm/½in thick. Arrange these in a gratin dish and sprinkle the layers with chopped shallots, nutmeg, salt and pepper as you go. Drizzle with cream, then bake in the oven for about 30 minutes or until the onions are crusty and the cream has evaporated into a small amount of thick sauce. Serve straight away.

Roasted Mushrooms with Pink Peppercorns, Chervil and Almonds

SERVES 6

Super-easy to prepare and strikingly delicious, this dish combines marinated then roasted mushrooms with fresh herbs, pink peppercorns and slivered almonds. If you do not have chervil, use fresh tarragon, parsley or chives, and if almonds are not in your larder use coarsely chopped hazelnuts, the pricier pine kernels, or omit them all and serve the mushrooms without any nuts. If pink peppercorns are either not available or prohibitive in price, the mushrooms will be delicious without them, too. Serve as a hot appetizer, a vegetarian supper dish, or a side dish for omnivores.

350–500 g/12–16 oz mature flat
   mushrooms
5–8 cloves garlic, chopped
4–6 tablespoons extra virgin olive oil
about 2 tablespoons balsamic vinegar

salt
3 tablespoons slivered almonds
1–2 teaspoons pink peppercorns
1 tablespoon chopped fresh chervil
   and/or tarragon, or chopped parsley

◆ Remove the stems from the mushrooms if they are tough; if not, just trim. Sprinkle the mushrooms with the garlic, olive oil, balsamic vinegar and salt to taste, and leave to marinate for 30 minutes. Preheat the oven to 200°C/400°F/Gas Mark 6.

◆ Meanwhile, lightly toast the almonds in a heavy ungreased frying pan over a medium-high heat, tossing and turning every few moments, until they are golden and lightly browned in spots. Remove from the heat and set aside.

◆ Arrange the mushrooms, gill sides up, in a baking dish with their marinade, and bake in the oven for 6–8 minutes or until they are browned on their gill sides, then turn them over and cook until the other side is lightly browned too and/or the mushrooms are just tender. Alternatively, cook under a hot grill.

◆ Serve sprinkled with the almonds, pink peppercorns and herbs.

Soy-Ginger Roasted Swedes

SERVES 6 as a side dish

Swedes are a sure symbol of warming winter eating, their pale orange flesh tasting slightly of turnip, slightly sweet like squash, as hearty as but lighter than a potato. Glazing swede with soy sauce and ginger gives East–West flavour and emphasises its down to earth, rooty nature.

500g/1lb swede, peeled and cut into
   chunks
2 tablespoons olive oil
2 teaspoons soy sauce, or to taste

1 tablespoon sugar
1 teaspoon chopped fresh ginger
3 cloves garlic, chopped

◆ Preheat the oven to 190°C/375°F/Gas Mark 5. Place the swede in a roasting tin, drizzle with oil, and roast for about 1 hour or until golden brown. Remove from the oven and toss with the soy sauce, sugar, ginger and garlic. Return to the oven and continue to bake for 10–15 minutes or until the vegetables are glazed. Serve hot.

Crispy Fried Celeriac Batons

SERVES 6

These crispy little batons look like chips but have a wonderful surprise inside of tender celeriac. Serve as a side dish; it's especially good with roast chicken.

1 celeriac root, trimmed of its knobby,
   earthy skin
salt and pepper
½ teaspoon paprika
1 clove garlic, chopped

175g/6oz flour
pure olive oil or bland vegetable oil, for
   frying
2 tablespoons chopped fresh parsley to
   serve (optional)

◆ Cut the celeriac into French-fry or baton shapes, then cook them in rapidly boiling salted water for 5–8 minutes or until they are just tender. Drain well (saving the liquid to use in a soup), let the celeriac cool slightly, then toss the strips first with a mixture of salt, pepper, paprika and garlic, then with flour, mixing them to coat well.

- Heat about 1cm/½in olive oil in a heavy frying pan and, when it begins to smoke, add the celeriac, taking care to shake off the excess flour. Cook until the celeriac is crisp and lightly browned, turning once or twice to brown evenly. Drain on absorbent kitchen paper and serve hot, sprinkled with parsley if desired.

Potato and Goats' Cheese Gratin

SERVES 6

Serve as a side dish with rare roasted lamb or as a main course, paired with a salad of flash-cooked green beans, black olives and ripe tomatoes.

1.1kg/2¼lb potatoes, preferably slightly
  waxy
90ml/3fl oz extra virgin olive oil
5–7 cloves garlic, chopped

125g/4oz goats' cheese log, sliced
salt and pepper
½–1 teaspoon herbes de Provence

- Parboil the whole, unpeeled potatoes until they are *al dente* but still too crunchy to eat. This should take 20–25 minutes, depending on the size of the potatoes; if they are on the smallish side, decrease the cooking time to about 15 minutes. Drain well and, when cool enough to handle, peel and slice. Preheat the oven to 190°C/375°F/Gas Mark 5.

- Sprinkle the bottom of a medium gratin dish with olive oil and some of the chopped garlic, then layer the potatoes and the goats' cheese in the dish, sprinkling them with garlic, salt, pepper, and herbes de Provence as you build the casserole, ending with a layer of goats' cheese and a drizzle of olive oil.

- Bake in the oven for about 40 minutes or until the top is golden and lightly crusted in places.

Sautéed New Potatoes with Garlic and Parsley

SERVES 6

This is classic bistro fare: sautéed tiny young potatoes, finished with a sprinkling of crushed garlic and parsley. Enjoy alongside anything hearty, such as roast chicken or sautéed escalopes of pork or beef (see page 104). In France, you would use a type of creamy textured, nutty-tasting luscious new potato called 'ratte'; in Britain choose Jersey, Cyprus or Egypt potatoes. As William Shakespeare reputedly said: 'Let the sky rain potatoes!'

500g/1lb tiny new potatoes
pinch each of salt and sugar
45g/1½oz butter
2–3 tablespoons vegetable oil

3 cloves garlic, chopped
salt and pepper
3 tablespoons chopped fresh parsley

- ◆ Cook the unpeeled potatoes in simmering water to cover, with a pinch of salt and sugar, for about 15 minutes or until they are half cooked. This will stabilize the starch and enable them to keep their shape and not absorb a huge quantity of oil as they brown.

- ◆ When the potatoes are cool enough to handle, slice them thinly lengthways, discarding the peel that slips off as you slice.

- ◆ Heat the butter and oil in a large heavy frying pan until the butter has melted and is lightly foaming. Add the potatoes and cook over a medium heat for 10–15 minutes, turning every so often, until the potatoes are golden brown.

- ◆ Combine the chopped garlic, salt, pepper and parsley in a mortar and pestle, and crush them lightly to extract most of their flavour and fragrance. Turn the potatoes out on to a warm plate or platter, and sprinkle with the garlic and parsley mixture. Eat straight away.

Opposite: Pacific Rim Salad (page 66)

Mediterranean Caper and Tomato 'Mash'

SERVES 6

Utterly savoury and comforting, this is captivating enough to eat as a main course with a spritely salad alongside, but well mannered enough to serve as a bed for something elegant and in dinner-party mode – thinly sliced lamb, or a bacon-wrapped fish fillet, perhaps.

1.25kg/2¼lb (about 6 large) floury potatoes, peeled and cut into chunks
pinch of sugar
4–6 tablespoons extra virgin or strong flavoured pure olive oil
6–8 cloves garlic, chopped
400g/14oz can chopped tomatoes
90g/3oz double cream

4–6 teaspoons capers, drained, then soaked in a little cold water for a few minutes, then drained again
¼ teaspoon oregano leaves (or more, to taste)
2–3 tablespoons fromage frais or Greek yogurt (optional)
pinch of crushed dried red chillies
salt and pepper

- Place the potatoes in a saucepan of lightly salted water. Add a pinch of sugar, cover and bring to the boil. Cook until the potatoes are just tender, then remove from the heat and drain.

- Meanwhile, heat 3–4 tablespoons olive oil in a frying pan and cook the garlic for a few moments until golden, then add the tomatoes (with their juices), and cook, stirring, over a medium-high heat until they are well reduced and thickened. The oil will have separated from the tomatoes and be a rich orange colour.

- Mash the potatoes with the cream, then stir in the tomato mixture, capers, oregano, fromage frais or yogurt, if using, a pinch of crushed red chillies, and salt and pepper to taste. Serve warm.

Opposite: French Country Soup with Berries (page 138)

Creamy Almond Risotto

SERVES 6

One of the most delightful things about entertaining is that it provides an excuse to make unusual dishes that one wouldn't otherwise have an opportunity to try. This almond risotto is a good example. It is rich and scented with almonds, the recipe a result of a super post-Christmas purchase of cut-price almonds and cream, combined with an eavesdropped conversation in the Paris Metro. Serve in bowls as a course on its own, garnished with a few chives or edible flowers.

100g/3½oz raw (untoasted) almonds, with their skins
30g/1oz butter
1 tablespoon vegetable oil
½ onion, chopped
3 cloves garlic, chopped
350g/12oz risotto rice
1.25 litres/2 pints hot vegetable or chicken stock

a few drops almond flavouring essence (about ⅛–¼ teaspoon, or to taste)
350ml/12fl oz single cream
75g/2½oz freshly grated Parmesan or Pecorino, or other grana-type cheese
coarsely ground black pepper to taste
salt (if needed)

- Coarsely cut up the almonds with a knife, then set aside.

- Heat the butter and oil in a large frying pan and lightly sauté the onion and half the garlic for 5–10 minutes or until softened. Stir in the rice and nuts, and cook for about 5 minutes or until the rice is lightly gilded with colour.

- Start adding the stock: stir in about 125ml/4fl oz and cook, stirring, until the rice absorbs the liquid, then repeat again and again, letting the rice absorb the liquid each time before adding more. After about 20 minutes your rice should be almost *al dente* but still just a little too crunchy to eat. Stir in the almond flavouring/essence and half the cream and cook, stirring, for about 5 minutes more, then add the rest of the cream and continue to cook, stirring, until the rice grains are *al dente* and the sauce creamy. If it is too thick, add a little hot water, stir it in, and cook together for a few more minutes.

- Remove from the heat, stir in the remaining garlic, cheese, black pepper, and salt if needed, and serve straight away.

Refried Beans with Bacon, Tomatoes and Melted Cheese

SERVES 6

Refried beans is actually a bit of a misnomer, as the beans are not even fried once, let alone twice. What they are is tender simmered beans, puréed with onions and flavouring ingredients, then cooked down into a deliciously lumpy paste with enough fat to keep it rich and smooth. Traditionally, it is lard that gives its heft to frijoles, but in these health-conscious days it is more likely to be vegetable oil. Bits of browned bacon, diced tomatoes, spices and melted cheese all enrich the dish and turn it from a bowl of beans into something substantial and more-ish.

2 tablespoons vegetable oil
1 onion, chopped
3–5 cloves garlic, chopped
250g/8oz bacon bits, derinded
1 teaspoon cumin seeds or ground cumin
½ teaspoon mild chillli powder (optional)
large pinch of dried oregano
400g/14oz can chopped tomatoes
1 x 470g/15oz can refried beans

1 x 470g/15oz can borlotti or pinto
   beans, drained
350g/12oz mild cheese, such as a
   Cheddar or mozzarella, diced
salt and black pepper
3–4 tablespoons each of chopped spring
   onions and chopped coriander leaves
12 flour or corn tortillas and sour cream
   or Greek yogurt to serve

- Heat the oil in a saucepan and lightly sauté the onion, garlic and bacon for 5–10 minutes or until golden brown in spots, then sprinkle with the cumin, mild chilli, if using, and oregano, and stir in the tomatoes with their juice. Cook over a high heat for a few minutes, then add the beans and break them up somewhat, mashing them a little. Cover and cook for 10 minutes over a medium-low heat, then scatter the cheese over the top, return the cover, and continue to cook for another 10 minutes or until the beans are thick and smooth but not burning on the bottom, and the cheese has melted. (If using mozzarella you will find it mercilessly stringy!)

- Taste for seasoning, sprinkle with spring onions and coriander, and serve with warm tortillas and a bowl of sour cream or Greek yogurt for each person to plop on as he or she desires.

'Little Havana' Spicy Black Beans

SERVES 6

Black beans, stewed with chilli and spices, are as festive as they are tasty, and make any meal seem like a party in the tropics. They are increasingly available and, like all beans and legumes, very affordable. They can be cooked ahead of time and kept for several days in the refrigerator, or for several months in the freezer.

250g/8oz black beans (see Note opposite)
2 litres/3¼ pints water
2 tablespoons olive oil
2 onions, chopped
8 cloves garlic, coarsely chopped
1 tablespoon paprika
2 teaspoons mild chilli powder (or, if available, ancho or New Mexico chilli powder)

½ teaspoon dried oregano
1 tablespoon ground cumin
400g/14oz can chopped tomatoes
1 vegetable stock cube, crumbled, and/or salt to taste
2 tablespoons chopped fresh coriander

- ◆ Soak the black beans overnight, or put them in a saucepan with the water and bring to the boil, then remove from the heat and leave to soak in their cooking water for 1 hour. Do not drain the beans, as their black inky colour and distinctive flavour will be drained away. Cook the beans over a medium-low heat for about 1½ hours or until they are very tender.

- ◆ Meanwhile, heat the oil in a frying pan and lightly sauté the onions for 5–10 minutes, or until softened. Add half the garlic and stir in the paprika, chilli powder, oregano and cumin. Cook for a few minutes, add the tomatoes (with their juice), then pour it all into the cooked black beans.

- ◆ Add the remaining garlic, stock cube or salt to taste to the beans with the coriander, and cook over a medium-high heat for 20–30 minutes or until the liquid has evaporated and thickened into a rich sauce. If the mixture is still too watery, raise the heat. Mash a few of the beans as you go along as this contributes to the richness of the sauce.

Note

There are three types of black beans available. The first are Chinese black beans, which are salted, soft, little beans used as a seasoning. You might find black kidney beans, which are black in colour but taste very similar to other kidney beans. The black beans I recommend are smallish and known sometimes as turtle beans. Several supermarkets/shops sell them both dried and in cans.

Barley with Moroccan Flavours

SERVES 6

In this dish, adapted from the Moroccan Jewish community, barley is cooked in a spicy stock. Enjoy it warm as a base for barbecued kebabs. Cool, it makes a lovely summer salad.

2 onions, chopped
3 tablespoons olive oil
½ green pepper or 1 courgette/¼ marrow or 1 carrot, diced
5 cloves garlic, chopped
1 tablespoon chopped fresh ginger
½–1 teaspoon each of ground turmeric, ground cumin and curry powder

1½ teaspoons each of paprika and mild chilli powder
¼ teaspoon each of cayenne pepper and coarsely ground black pepper
625g/1¼lb barley
1 litre/32fl oz vegetable stock
3 tablespoons tomato paste

◆ Lightly sauté the onions in the olive oil with the green pepper, courgette, marrow or carrot for about 10 minutes or until the vegetables are softened. Sprinkle in half the garlic and ginger, cook for a few minutes, then add the turmeric, cumin, curry powder, paprika, mild chilli powder, cayenne pepper and coarsely ground black pepper. Cook, stirring, for a few moments, then add the barley and vegetable stock.

◆ Bring to the boil, then reduce the heat, cover, and simmer for 20–30 minutes or until the barley is *al dente* and almost all of the liquid has been absorbed. Stir in the tomato paste and the remaining garlic and ginger, and return to the heat. Continue to cook for a further 5–10 minutes or until all the liquid has been absorbed and the barley is tender. Serve warm or at room temperature.

Salsas, Chutneys and Relishes

8

Salsas, Chutneys and Relishes

...a bowl of spicy,

tangy, chunky or

smooth sauce, full of

bright flavour...

Salsas, Chutneys and Relishes

A **BOWL** of spicy, tangy, chunky or smooth sauce, full of bright flavour, eaten in dabs as desired can transform simple food to extraordinary.

The easiest-to-throw-together concoction of diced chillies with tomatoes, onions, garlic, salt and pepper makes a classic of the Mexican kitchen. Raitas, Indian salsas based on yogurt, add great taste, texture and vitality dabbed on to rice, flat-breads, curried vegetables or grilled meats.

Even simply chopping up tomatoes and dressing them with olive oil and garlic makes a sauce to remember. Spoon it over pasta, grilled fish or humble bread. It costs pennies if tomatoes are in seasonal abundance, and gives great flavour and health.

Avocado and Sweetcorn Salsa

SERVES **Makes enough for about 6**

Though avocados are imported, they too have their season, when they can be reasonable or even downright cheap. To choose a good avocado, do not press on the sides; that only bruises them. Instead, lightly press on the flesh at the top of the fruit – if it 'gives' slightly it is ready; if it is soft, it is past it.

There is so much more to do with a luscious avocado than make guacamole – though homemade guacamole *is* wonderful. This salsa is pretty: pale green avocado, yellow sweetcorn, dark green coriander and nubbins of red tomato. It is scented with lime and delicious. Enjoy with a stack of warm tortillas or any spicy food cooked on the barbecue.

125g/4oz sweetcorn kernels (fresh or frozen and cooked, or canned, drained)
3–4 ripe tomatoes, diced
½ fresh green chilli, chopped
1 small to medium onion, chopped

2 cloves garlic, chopped
2 tablespoons chopped fresh coriander
2 avocados, preferably of the thick-skinned Hass variety
2 tablespoons lime juice
salt

◆ Combine the sweetcorn with the tomatoes, chilli, onion, garlic and coriander. Halve, stone and peel the avocados and cut into bite-sized pieces. Add to the sweetcorn mixture with the lime juice, and season with salt to taste. Toss gently together.

GARLIC GALORE

Don't only think of France, Italy and other Mediterranean regions as being the garlic capitals of the world – our own Isle of Wight has a festival each summer. When the fresh crop of garlic is in the shops, have your own garlic festival to celebrate: make Provençal Garlic Soup (page 61), garlicky marinated barbecued meat with any raita or yogurt, garlic-dressed salad leaves, and/or Potato and Goats' Cheese Gratin (page 119).

Sicilian Fresh Tomato Sauce

SERVES **Makes enough for about 6**

Delicious on anything toasted or grilled, such as bruschetta, fish, vegetables, meat or chicken.

500g/1lb very ripe sweet tomatoes, diced (including their juices)
3 cloves garlic, chopped
4–5 tablespoons olive oil
salt, pepper, sugar and crushed dried red chillies, to taste

1 teaspoon dried oregano leaves or 2 teaspoons chopped fresh oregano
1 tablespoon vinegar

◆ Combine all the ingredients and leave to stand until ready to serve.

VARIATION

For a simple pasta salad, add the fresh tomato sauce to chunky *al dente* pasta (such as penne), and toss together with a handful of chopped red onion, diced black olives, sweet basil, parsley and/or mint.

Preserved Lemons

SERVES **Makes enough to fill 2 × 300–350ml/ 10–12fl oz jars**

Throughout Morocco and in the markets of France you will find preserved lemons resting in bowls of honey-coloured lemon juice, small, round and ochre-yellow in colour. Having a jar in your refrigerator means you always have a big dose of flavour to add to almost anything.

Preserved lemons are easy to make and, as long as you use enough salt, there should be no problem with them keeping for 2–3 months.

I tend to make preserved lemons with whichever lemons I have available, and I cut them up, first because it is easier and, second, because it makes the pickling process much quicker. I make several jars at a time, then perhaps a month or two later I repeat the process. This way I have a constant supply of preserved lemons.

Use in salad dressings or marinades, or try my secret passion, a small amount of preserved lemons on buttered pasta. Try Tomato and Preserved Lemon Salsa (page 46) too. Original and exciting flavours!

salt

about 12 lemons (preferably unwaxed), well cleaned

about 125ml/4fl oz boiling water (or more, as needed)

about 125ml/4fl oz bottled lemon juice (or more, as needed)

- ◆ You will need two 300–350ml/10–12fl oz jars with tight-fitting lids. To prepare them, wash them thoroughly, then place a knife or other metal utensil in each jar and pour boiling water into them. Alternatively, you can wash them in a dishwasher using a very hot setting, or submerge them in boiling water if they are proper preserving jars and can take the heat without breaking.

- ◆ Place a heaped teaspoon of salt in the bottom of each jar. Cut two or three of the lemons towards their centres in three or four places, making what are essentially large gashes in each fruit. Fill each of these with a teaspoon or more of salt. Cut the remaining lemons into quarters or wedges.

- ◆ Place the salt-stuffed lemons in the jars, then add the lemon wedges to fill. Pour boiling water over the lemons, then add an equal amount of lemon juice. The liquid should reach about 5mm (¼in) from the top of each jar.

- ◆ Place 1 tablespoon salt on top of the lemons in each jar, then seal with the lids. Leave in a cool place to season for about a week, then transfer to the refrigerator, where they should keep for 2–3 months. The lemons will darken slightly and the juices they are pickled in will thicken, becoming almost honey-like.

Vietnamese Lime or Lemon Dipping Sauce

SERVES Makes 3–4 tablespoons; enough for about 6 people

Feisty, tart and utterly fresh, Vietnamese lime or lemon sauce is drizzled on to all sorts of dishes at the table, in addition to or in place of fish sauce or hot pepper seasoning. It is simply salted lemon or lime juice, but its brighter flavour belies its simplicity. Serve with noodles, or anything with a Far-Eastern flavour. The sauce will depend upon the type of citrus you use – exotic limes, such as the orange-coloured Rangpur, are delicious, but plain lemon juice from a bottle is very cheap.

3–4 tablespoons lime or lemon juice
1 teaspoon salt

◆ Combine the two ingredients and mix well to dissolve the salt. Serve as desired.

Roasted Tomatoes

This is a terrific thing to do with tomatoes that are in plentiful abundance. Roasted tomatoes are intensely flavoured and a marvellous change from ordinary sliced tomato salad or simmered tomato sauce.

1.5kg/3lb tomatoes
1 tablespoon olive oil
sprinkle of salt, sugar and dried oregano

◆ Preheat the oven to 180°C/350°F/Gas Mark 4. Fill a casserole or baking dish with a single layer of ripe tomatoes, each with a shallow cross carved into its stem end. Drizzle olive oil and a sprinkling of sugar, salt and oregano over the tomatoes and roast in the oven for 30–45 minutes. Remove from the oven and leave for several hours or overnight to cool (their juices will thicken).

SERVING IDEAS

◆ As an appetizer, sprinkled with chopped garlic, balsamic vinegar and chopped fresh basil. Let each person remove the skin and season the tomatoes as desired.

◆ For roasted tomato coulis, remove the skins and squeeze them to extract all the juices. Dice the tomatoes, mix them with their juices, and season with salt, pepper, olive oil, chopped garlic and basil or other herbs as desired.

◆ Roasted Tomato Couscous and Green Beans: toss peeled and diced roasted tomatoes into cooked couscous along with some roughly chopped *al dente* green beans and lots of chopped garlic and olive oil. Add salt and pepper to taste.

◆ Roasted Tomato Soup with Pastina or Orzo: stir peeled and chopped roasted tomatoes into hot stock (either vegetable or chicken), add lots of cooked pastina or orzo, season with chopped garlic to taste, and serve with a dab of pesto and a drizzle of olive oil.

◆ Roasted Tomato and Asparagus 'Pizzette': if asparagus is still available, cook a few spears until *al dente*, then drain and dice. Arrange on a flour tortilla, along with diced roasted tomatoes, a sprinkling of garlic, grated or diced Fontina or mozzarella, Parmesan, olive oil and chopped fresh oregano. Grill until the cheese melts and sizzles. Serve hot, sprinkled with more fresh oregano, basil or rosemary.

Desserts
and
Puddings

9

Desserts and Puddings

...crunchy, softly squishy, crisp, spicy; a handful of sweet indulgent offerings...

Desserts and Puddings

USUALLY serve fruit, sorbet or maybe a tart as dessert for dinner parties, since I find most rich puddings demanding to prepare and very expensive. True, I adore chocolate and like to indulge, but after a big dinner I'm too full to appreciate the pudding. (If I'm eating chocolate, I like to give it my complete attention.)

However, many people feel they have not truly been fêted if there is no special pudding, so I have included a handful of sweet indulgent offerings in this chapter. And, even if I do serve a light and vivacious fruit dessert, I always pass around a plate of rich decadent chocolates for those who nurture a sweet tooth.

'Instant' Melon Ice with Blackberry Coulis

SERVES 6

This melon ice is a marvellous thing to do with a melon that is at its peak of flavour but mushy rather than firm, as bargain melons often are. Freeze the chunks for up to a month, then take them out of the freezer and whirl them up into a nearly instant sorbet. For this technique you do need a food processor, but if you haven't got one make the ice in the more traditional way: purée the fruit, flavour the mixture, then freeze it and scrape the fruit purée into a light icy granita as it freezes.

2 ripe, sweet and fragrant, small to
   medium melons, or 1 larger one,
   peeled and seeded
caster sugar to taste
juice of ½ lemon or lime

250g/8oz blackberries, cleaned
1–2 tablespoons liqueur (any berry
   liqueur is fine) or 1 teaspoon raspberry
   or balsamic vinegar

◆ Cut the melon into bite-sized pieces, then arrange them on a cling-film-covered baking sheet. Freeze until they are firm, then take the melon chunks from the baking sheet and put them in a plastic bag. Seal well and return to the freezer. They should keep nicely for up to about a month this way. To make the ice, whirl the frozen melon pieces in a food processor with sugar and citrus juice to taste. Pour into a bowl and keep in the freezer while you make the blackberry coulis. Whirl the blackberries in a food processor with sugar and liqueur or vinegar to taste.

◆ Serve the melon ice in individual bowls or goblets drizzled with blackberry coulis.

French Country Soup of Strawberries and Peaches

SERVES 6

Fruit and wine – a simple countryside treat from the vineyard regions of France and Italy. You can vary it endlessly: use red instead of white wine, or bubbly with a dash of liqueur, or you can use less wine so that it is less a soup and more a compote.

If the season is rich with soft fruit and berries, omit the peaches and add raspberries, currants, blackberries – whichever luscious berry is available; if there are no berries, make the soup with all peaches and/or nectarines, or mangoes.

250–350g/8–12oz strawberries, hulled
3 ripe peaches (white, yellow or a combination of both), or nectarines
500ml/16fl oz dry or semi-sweet white wine

3 tablespoons sugar, or to taste
1 teaspoon orange flower water or grated orange zest
a few strips of fresh mint to decorate (optional)

◆ Clean the strawberries and halve or slice them. Peel (if preferred) and stone the peaches, and cut into bite-sized pieces, then toss them with the strawberries, wine, sugar and orange flower water or zest. Chill until ready to serve, decorated with sprigs of mint, if liked.

Sardinian Red Wine Prunes or Figs

SERVES 6

Prunes or dried figs simmered in sweet red wine are delicious, especially in winter when other fruits are costly and scarce, and you're likely to have some left-over wine from holiday entertaining. Serve with a scoop or two of vanilla ice cream if you like.

350g/12oz dried figs or stoneless
prunes
250ml/8fl oz each of dry red wine and
water

60–90g/2–3oz sugar, or to taste
1 stick cinnamon (optional)
juice of ¼ lemon
juice of ¼ orange

◆ Combine all the ingredients in a saucepan and bring to the boil. Reduce the heat to medium-low and simmer for 10–15 minutes or until the fruit plumps up and the liquid reduces by about half. Leave to cool at room temperature before serving.

Roasted Peaches or Nectarines with Amaretti Crumbs

SERVES 6

In high summer, a dessert like this is welcome. Enjoy it slightly warm, accompanied by cream, sorbet, or Greek yogurt.

8–10 ripe peaches or nectarines
12–16 amaretti biscuits, crumbled
2 tablespoons sugar, or to taste

a few drops of brandy and/or almond
essence/flavouring
a sprinkling of ground cinnamon
30g/1oz butter

◆ Preheat the oven to 200°C/400°F/Gas Mark 6. To peel the peaches, if using, cut a cross in the skin at the stem end of each one, then plunge them into boiling water for a few seconds. Remove and place immediately in cold water. The skins should slip off easily. If using nectarines, I tend to leave the skins on.

◆ Stone the fruit, then slice into a shallow baking dish. Sprinkle with about half the amaretti crumbs and half the sugar, a few drops of brandy or almond essence and some cinnamon. Toss together, then sprinkle the top with the remaining amaretti crumbs and sugar, and dot with the butter. Cover and bake in the oven for about 15 minutes, then remove the covering and bake for a further 5–10 minutes or until the top is lightly browned. Serve warm or at room temperature.

Pear Frangipane Tart

SERVES 6

In autumn, when pears are in cheap abundance, this is a marvellous tart to make; it is also delicious prepared with peaches or apricots.

350g/12oz shortcrust pastry (bought or homemade)
100g/3½oz ground almonds
1 egg, lightly beaten

125–175g/4–6oz sugar, or to taste
almond essence flavouring to taste
3 ripe but firm pears

- Preheat the oven to 180°C/350°F/Gas Mark 4.

- Roll out the pastry to 2.5–5mm/⅛–¼in thick and lay it out on a baking sheet. Combine the almonds with the egg, all but about 2 tablespoons sugar and about ½ teaspoon almond essence, then spoon it evenly over the pastry, leaving a border of about 2.5cm/1in around the edges. Fold the edges over to enclose the almond paste.

- Core the pears, peel them if preferred, and cut into slices. Arrange them over the top of the almond paste and sprinkle with the remaining sugar. Sprinkle a few drops of almond essence evenly over the sugared pears.

- Bake in the oven for 25–30 minutes or until the pastry is golden and the top sizzling hot and speckled with brown caramelized sugar. Serve hot or leave to cool.

MAKE YOUR TRIPS ABROAD PAY OFF

Spirits and wine are usually a fraction of the cost in other countries. Bring back the odd bottle of brandy, Pernod, liqueur or *eau de vie* to add sparkle to your desserts for a pittance. Even a simple fruit salad is transformed with a splash of something so luxurious.

Pears Poached in White Wine and Lemon

SERVES 6

This is a good dish to make use of pears that are too hard to eat raw. Though this recipe is Italian, similar dishes are eaten throughout the Mediterranean and Europe – France and Spain, for instance – or wherever pears and lemons grow and grapes are crushed into wine. It is a light dessert, perfect to end a hearty meal; for an indulgent enrichment, add a dollop of crème fraîche to each plate.

6 firm, slightly underripe pears   175g/6oz sugar, or to taste
2 lemons   500ml/16fl oz dry white wine

- Peel the pears but leave the stems attached. I do not bother to remove the cores, figuring that the pears stay together better with the cores in place, and that eaters can nibble around the cores. Place the pears, standing up, in a heavy saucepan.

- Remove the rind of one lemon with a vegetable peeler, keeping it in strips as long and wide as you can make them. Place in the pan with the pears, and add half the lemon juice, the sugar, wine and cold water to cover. Bring to the boil, then reduce the heat, cover, and cook for 15–20 minutes, turning the pears every so often, until they are just tender. Add a little more sugar during the cooking, to taste. Remove the pears from the syrup and boil the syrup down, adding water as it cooks, until the mixture is about 345ml/11fl oz in volume and the lemon rind is lightly candied.

- Squeeze the juice from the remaining lemon into the syrup, and pour over the pears. Serve warm, cool or chilled, as preferred.

Caramel, Apple and Sultana Bread Pudding

SERVES 6–8

This is actually much less rich than many bread puddings that ooze butter and cream. This is an elegant little pudding, studded with sultanas, sautéed apples, and with a puddle of caramel at the bottom. Each bite is crunchy, softly squishy, crisp and spicy at the same time. As for whether or not to trim the crusts from the bread, the choice is yours. Most recipes call for it, but I rather like the chewy little bits of crust and leave them on. The apple season is so glorious, and this pudding is a very good way to enjoy it. If you like, it can be reheated in the microwave.

For the caramel
250g/8oz sugar
90ml/3fl oz water

For the pudding
3 large tart apples, such as Granny
    Smiths, cored but unpeeled
45g/1½oz butter

400–500g/14–16oz slightly stale, sliced
    white bread, each slice cut into
    quarters
4–5 tablespoons sultanas
1–2 teaspoons ground cinnamon
900ml/1½ pints milk
3–4 eggs, lightly beaten
250g/8oz sugar

- ◆ To make the caramel, put the sugar and water in a small saucepan and heat gently, stirring, over a medium-low heat, until the sugar dissolves. Raise the heat, stop stirring and bring to the boil. Do not stir, but every so often either brush the sides of the pan with a wet pastry brush or drizzle a small amount of water down the sides with a spoon to prevent the caramel crystallizing. Continue boiling until the syrup turns a richly dark amber colour, then remove from the heat and pour into a large, round baking dish (30cm/12in diameter, 10cm/4in deep) or a rectangular dish (38 × 25cm/15 × 10in, 10cm/4in deep). Swirl the caramel around to coat both the bottom and sides of the dish, and leave to cool.

- ◆ Cut the apples into 5 mm/¼in slices. Heat 30g/1oz of the butter in a frying pan and lightly sauté the apples for 5–10 minutes or until golden brown and slightly softened. Remove from the heat. Layer half the apples in the caramel-lined baking dish and cover with about a third of the bread and a sprinkling of sultanas and half the cinnamon. Repeat, ending with a layer of bread.

- Mix the milk with the eggs and all but 1 tablespoon of the sugar. Pour this over the pudding, then sprinkle the top with the remaining cinnamon. Dot with the remaining butter and sprinkle with the remaining sugar. Leave to stand for about 30 minutes to allow the bread to absorb the milk and egg mixture.

- Preheat the oven to 180°C/350°F/Gas Mark 4 and bake the pudding for about 45 minutes or until the top is golden and crusty, and the inside still slightly custardy. Serve warm.

Punjabi Creamy Carrot and Rice Pudding

SERVES 6–8

This pudding is a sweet creamy mixture of rice and carrots, best eaten in the winter when carrots are in season. It is a festive dessert, eaten at parties, festivals and holiday gatherings. It is also very rich – I have made it without the double cream and it was still good. A spoonful of the pudding is wonderful resting in a puddle of bright red raspberry purée.

250g/8oz rice (preferably basmati)
1.5 litre/1½ pints full cream
185g/6oz double cream
1.1kg/2¼lb carrots, grated
250g/8oz sugar, or to taste
4–5 cardamom pods

6–8 heaped tablespoons desiccated coconut
6–8 tablespoons coarsely chopped almonds or a dash or two of almond essence flavouring

- Soak the rice in cold water to cover for about 2.5cm/1in. Leave for about 30 minutes, then drain.

- Put the rice in a saucepan with the milk, cream, carrots, sugar, cardamom, coconut and chopped almonds, if using. Bring to the boil, then reduce the heat and cook over a low heat for 20–30 minutes, stirring as often as you can, until the rice is very tender and the whole is pudding-like, thick and delicious. Add the almond essence or flavouring, if using. Turn into a bowl and chill before serving.

Ice Cream Sundae with Bunuelos and Coffee Syrup

SERVES 6

Boiling sugar to make a simple syrup, then combining it with leftover brewed coffee gives you the coffee sauce for this sundae.

Bunuelos are crispy deep-fried biscuits, a traditional Mexican and New Mexican treat. Using flour tortillas is an easy short-cut, and leftover stale ones are best of all. Save the few scraggly ends of tortillas you have after a night of Mexican food and stash them in your freezer.

For the coffee syrup
250g/8oz demerara or half demerara
    and half dark brown soft sugar
250ml/8fl oz water
250ml/8fl oz strong brewed coffee
    (leftover is fine)
½ teaspoon vanilla essence/flavouring
1 tablespoon brandy or whisky (optional)

For the bunuelos
3 flour tortillas
vegetable oil for frying
3 tablespoons caster sugar
3 tablespoons ground cinnamon

To serve
high quality ice cream, preferably praline
    crunch or dark chocolate

- To make the syrup, combine the sugar with the water in a small saucepan and bring to the boil, then reduce the heat to medium and cook for 10 minutes. Stir in the brewed coffee and continue to cook until the mixture is slightly syrupy. Remove from the heat and add the vanilla and, if using, the brandy or whisky. Leave to cool.

- Meanwhile, to make the bunuelos, cut each tortilla into 6–8 wedges. Pour about 7.5cm/3in oil into a wok or deep frying pan and heat until it is just smoking. Gently drop in the tortilla wedges, a few at a time, and cook on both sides until golden (not brown), then remove and drain on an absorbent kitchen paper. Combine the sugar and cinnamon and mix well, then shake generously over the tortilla wedges to coat well. Set aside.

- Arrange scoops of ice cream on individual plates or in sundae dishes. Drizzle with the coffee syrup, decorate with wedges of bunuelos, and serve at once.

Frozen Citrus Rounds

SERVES 6

These crisp, refreshing little titbits are deceivingly simple to prepare. When you eat them, you bite through both citrus rind and skin as well as fruit. They are very refreshing after a spicy meal, such as Indian or Mexican food.

1 lime
1 lemon
1 orange
sugar for sprinkling

- Slice the fruit very thinly, about 2.5mm/⅛in-thick, removing any pips you can. Cover a baking sheet with cling-film and place the citrus slices on it, taking care that they do not touch each other. Sprinkle generously with sugar and freeze until they are quite hard.

- Frozen fruit slices can be stored for up to a month in a well-sealed plastic bag in the freezer, though they might tend to stick to each other.

SOMETHING FOR NOTHING: CITRUS ZEST!

Be sure you either use unsprayed citrus fruit or you wash it well if you do not know. To anything that needs a hint of pure unadulterated splendid citrus flavour simply add a scraping of lime, orange, lemon or grapefruit zest (the coloured part of the rind). Use either the small holes of a grater or a special little gizmo called a 'zester' to remove the zest only from the fruit.

Chocolate-covered Sorbet Petits Fours

SERVES 6

These tasty little morsels are sweet enough to delight but small enough for almost anyone to enjoy, no matter how full they feel at the end of the meal. The chocolate is deliciously bitter-sweet, the sorbet filling refreshing. Since a great part of their charm is their freshness, serve as soon after making as you can. Even though they are frozen, I would serve them within a day or two rather than leaving them in the freezer for too long. Choose a good quality, not too sweet, fruit sorbet, preferably one that is all fruit without added sugar; I like raspberry best.

600ml/1 pint good-quality fruit sorbet
200g/7oz plain chocolate

2 tablespoons single cream or 30g/1oz
butter

- Cut the sorbet into tiny bite-sized cubes and place them on a cling-film-lined baking sheet. Stick a cocktail stick into each one to form a little handle, and refreeze until very hard.

- Melt the chocolate with the cream or butter, using a double boiler or a heatproof bowl over a saucepan of simmering water. Keep warm. Dip the frozen sorbet bites into the hot chocolate and return to the freezer; keep them there until ready to serve.

SUMMER BERRIES WITH BERRY SAUCE

When you have an abundance of berries, and they are ripe and cheap but some are going soft and slightly squishy, though they are still very fragrant and delicious, this way of preparing them makes an excellent treat. Divide your berries up (you can use any type you like, or a selection of several) and place all the soft ones in one pile. You want about half and half. Trim the soft berries of any spots that are going off, then purée them, sweeten them to taste, and add a dash of either balsamic vinegar, lemon juice, red wine or a berry-flavoured liqueur. Serve the whole berries on a plate with some of the purée puddled around them. Decorate, if you like, with mint leaves, and a dollop of whipped cream or ice cream.

Frozen Banana 'Bites' with Warm Chocolate Fondue

SERVES 6

An adaptation of a childhood treat I adored: frozen bananas on a stick, eaten while walking along the Santa Cruz California boardwalk. Here the bananas are no longer street food, but rather civilized little bites, dipped into a warm chocolate sauce. You could, if you liked, accompany it with a saucerful of coarsely chopped unsalted almonds, for dipping the chocolate covered morsels.

6 ripe but firm bananas
200g/7oz plain chocolate

3–5 tablespoons milk or single cream

- Peel and slice the bananas, and arrange them on a cling-film-wrapped or covered metal serving tray. (It needs to be metal as metal keeps cold when serving, and also won't crack or break in the freezer.) Put the tray of banana slices in the freezer. The time they take to freeze will depend on your freezer, but no less than 3 hours.

- When ready to serve, break the chocolate into bite-sized pieces and warm it, together with the milk or cream, either in a saucepan on the hob or in the microwave, until melted, stirring every so often to keep it smooth. If you can, transfer the melted chocolate sauce to a fondue pot and keep it warm at the table. If you can't do this, rewarm the sauce every so often for just a moment or two, then return it to the table.

- Bring the frozen banana bites to the table on their cling-film-wrapped tray, and let each person spear a frozen banana morsel with a cocktail stick or fork (ordinary or fondue). Quickly dip the banana bites into the hot chocolate sauce, wait a moment for the chocolate to firm up, then pop into the mouth and enjoy!

VARIATION

In the strawberry season, freeze whole strawberries in place of banana slices.

Upside-down Banana Tart

SERVES 6

This is inspired by the famous tarte Tatin of France, that luscious upside-down pie of caramelized apples topped with a crust of puff pastry. Here the fruit is banana instead of apple, and bought puff pastry makes it a doddle to put together.

You can vary this little pie: uncaramelized bananas make a paler, lighter filling (less attractive to the eye, but deliciously sweet and banana-y); ripe bananas make a much more liquid, juicier filling. Both are different, and both good. Alternatively, you can omit the sugar and add chocolate instead, breaking up a bar of plain chocolate and adding it to the bananas. Eat as you would a warm pudding, digging through the crisp topping to the cache of molten fruit underneath.

30–45g/1–1½oz unsalted butter
125–175g/4–6oz sugar, to taste, plus a little extra for sprinkling
6 ripe but firm bananas, peeled and sliced

juice of ¼–½ lemon
350g/12oz puff pastry (bought is fine)

- Preheat the oven to 200°C/400°F/Gas Mark 6. Put the butter and sugar in a large heavy frying pan with an ovenproof handle, and warm over a low to medium heat until it turns golden in colour, stirring and swirling every so often. Remove from the heat and layer the bananas on top of this melted sugar mixture. Squeeze the lemon juice over the top.

- Roll out the pastry to a thin round layer, about 5cm/2in larger than the diameter of the pan. Place it on top of the bananas, then fold the edges over the side of the pan and crimp to seal it. Pierce the pastry all over and sprinkle with sugar to taste.

- Bake in the oven for about 30 minutes or until the pastry is a light golden brown. Serve warm.

Seriously Good Chocolate Chunk Cookies

SERVES 6

Good cookies are not cheap to make, but they are so very good, it's worth the splurge and cutting back in other areas. Here are my current favourite cookies. Serve them for a party or at teatime on a plate, but for a more formal dinner-party presentation, serve them filled with a slab of chocolate or vanilla ice cream.

125g/4oz butter, softened
125g/4oz demerara sugar
125g/4oz granulated sugar
1 egg, lightly beaten
1 teaspoon vanilla essence/flavouring

pinch of salt
175g/6oz self-raising flour
½ teaspoon bicarbonate of soda
200g/7oz plain chocolate, broken into
   chunks

◆ Preheat the oven to 180°C/350°F/Gas Mark 4. Combine the butter with the brown and granulated sugars, and mix well, then beat in the egg, vanilla and salt. Stir in the self-raising flour and bicarbonate of soda, and mix only until the mixture is of the consistency of a softish dough. Mix in the chocolate chunks.

◆ Spoon the dough in dollops of 1–2 tablespoons each on to a greased baking sheet (or a baking sheet lined with baking parchment), allowing enough space between the blobs of dough for the cookies to spread out. If they don't have enough room you will end up with one huge cookie, which isn't terrible and won't ruin your delight: simply cut it up while still hot.

◆ Bake in the oven for 10–15 minutes or until the dough spreads out and the cookies are light golden brown. The chocolate will have melted and be alluringly gooey. Take care not to burn your tongue when you grab a little taste!

◆ Leave the cookies for a moment on the baking sheet, then remove and arrange on a wire rack to cool.

Index